DATE DUE

MERRILL'S INTERNATIONAL EDUCATION SERIES

Under the Editorship of
KIMBALL WILES
*Late Dean of the College of Education
University of Florida*

Fostering
**Educational
Change**

Jack R. Frymier
The Ohio State University

Fostering
Educational
Change

CHARLES E. MERRILL PUBLISHING COMPANY
Columbus, Ohio   *A Bell & Howell Company*

Copyright © 1969, by CHARLES E. MERRILL PUBLISHING COMPANY, Columbus, Ohio. All rights reserved. No part of this book may be reproduced in any form, by mimeograph or other means, without the written permission of the publisher.

Standard Book Number: 675-09532-8

Library of Congress Catalog Card Number: 69-13720

1 2 3 4 5 6 7 8 9 10 —
73 72 71 70 69 68

PRINTED IN THE UNITED STATES OF AMERICA

To
JILL and KAY and MACK
Who have lived and learned within the system as it is

PREFACE

This is a little book, and it is meant to be read at one sitting. What is said here is quite straightforward: the educational "system" must be changed. But changing an institutionalized system is not so easily done.

This book probes some of the theoretical aspects of the "system" and of "change." The issues are controversial and often generate heated discussion. Certainly, many who have reacted to the ideas presented here have been uncomfortable with the proposed rationale—but the discussion has always been lively. Hopefully, the reader will find the basic ideas stimulating and perhaps ultimately useful.

Many persons have read all or parts of the manuscript and have made helpful criticisms: William Alexander, L. O. Andrews, Leslee Bishop, James Boyer, Donald Bond, Bob Burton Brown, O. L. Davis, Jr., Kelly Duncan, H. C. Hawn, Paul Klohr, Sam Leles, John Ramseyer, James Raths, and Kimball Wiles. Walcott Beatty, David Clark, Donald Dowd, Egon Guba, Earl Kelley, Karl Openshaw, Arliss Roaden and Barbara Thomson have discussed some of the themes of the book with me at various times, and all have contributed immeasurably to the development of the rationale—most of all when they disagreed.

Finally, I am especially grateful to the many graduate students who have permitted me to "test out" these ideas in my teaching. More than once, I have been "nailed to the wall" by their unerring questions and carefully developed logic. Their feedback has enabled me to modify the ideas and to evolve a new and better concept.

To Mrs. Beverly Wells I am indebted for preparing the manuscript in final copy.

JACK R. FRYMIER

Columbus, Ohio

Contents

Chapter One
THE NECESSITY FOR EDUCATIONAL CHANGE 1

Introduction	1
Forces Affecting Educational Change	2
The Response to the Forces	4
The Problem Defined	9

Chapter Two
PREVIOUS EFFORTS AT EDUCATIONAL CHANGE 11

Introduction	11
Hypotheses Regarding Educational Change	11
The Testing of These Hypotheses	17
Why These Hypotheses Have Failed	20
Summary	25

Chapter Three
THE SOCIAL SYSTEMS CONCEPT AND EDUCATION 27

Introduction	27
The Social Systems Concept	27
The Power of the Systems Concept	31
The Inadequacy in the Educational System	35
The Educational Dilemma	41
Summary	44

Chapter Four

UNTANGLING THE THEORETICAL DIMENSIONS 46

Introduction 46
The Theoretical Dimensions 47
Reconceptualizing the
 Educational System 53

Chapter Five

PROPOSITIONS FOR EDUCATIONAL CHANGE 62

Introduction 62
Integrity of the Educational System 63
Redundancy of Evaluative Function 65
Some Propositions Regarding Change 70
Some Final Observations
 Regarding Change 81

Appendix A

ANNOTATED BIBLIOGRAPHY 85

Appendix B

A PLAN FOR ORGANIZING A COLLEGE WITHIN A UNIVERSITY 171

Appendix C

ESTABLISHING A PROFESSIONAL PRACTICES BOARD 183

Appendix D

ESTABLISHING CURRICULUM RESEARCH COUNCILS 193

Index **201**

I am not an advocate for frequent changes in laws and constitutions, but laws and institutions must go hand in hand with the progress of the human mind. As that becomes more developed, more enlightened, as new discoveries are made, new truths discovered and manners and opinions change with the change of circumstances, institutions must advance also to keep pace with the times. We might as well require a man to wear still the coat which fitted him when a boy as civilized society to remain ever under the regimen of their barbarous ancesters.
THOMAS JEFFERSON

Chapter One

The Necessity for Educational Change

INTRODUCTION

An ancient Greek maintained that "no man can step into the same river twice." The river is always changing; so is life. Those of us who live in the latter half of the twentieth century have come to accept the inevitability of social change, and the years ahead promise even greater changes in still shorter periods of time.

Out of this fantastic flux, a problem is born: Can we—will we—find ways of coping with and harnessing for human good the potential power inherent in social change? Change can be undesirable. Just as the wild growth of cancerous tissue within the human organism represents an extensive but negative organic change, so can some of the social changes presently underway run amuk and destroy the social fabric upon which they feed.

The purpose of this book is to explore both the dynamics and problems of one particular kind of social change: educational change. As a starting point, this chapter will first outline a series of known conditions, and second, describe some of the more important reactions to these conditions in the attempt to build a case for the imperative need for orderly and rational educational change today. The ideas set forth are all well known, but it seems appropriate to include them here as a conceptual base for the discussion which follows.

FORCES AFFECTING EDUCATIONAL CHANGE

Many factors affect change in education, but only three will be discussed at any length here: the population explosion, the explosion of knowledge, and conflicting ideologies with their threat of nuclear war. These conditions work to induce social change. They are probably the must crucial and most pervasive factors affecting educational change today.

There Are More People

The world's population has been increasing at a phenomenal rate. There were fewer than five million people in the United States when our nation was founded less than 200 years ago. At the time of the Civil War, less than 30 million people lived within our national borders. By 1900, that number had increased to 75 million, and by 1950, to over 150 million. Today, the population of America approaches the 200-million mark, and sociologists estimate that by the year 2000, there will be more than 300 million people living within the United States alone. At the same rate of increase, there will be more than half a billion inhabitants of our great land by 2050, and at least some of those youngsters now in school will be living then.

Added to this almost unbelievable increase in numbers of people, there are major population shifts in terms of the proportion of people falling within certain age brackets. Even though the total population of the United States has increased, the proportion of persons age 20 to 65 has decreased appreciably since 1920. Since this age group constitutes the "working force" and the production segment of society, a greater proportion of dependent people (youngsters and oldsters) must be provided for by the total social order than ever before. The United Nations has

The Necessity for Educational Change 3

compiled figures for the past few decades, which give the world's population in 1920 as 1,810 million; in 1930 as 2,013 million; in 1940 as 2,246 million; in 1950 as 2,476 million; and in 1956 as 2,734 million. The U.N. estimates that world population is now growing at the approximate rate of 44 million a year, and the rate of increase is still accelerating.

The "population explosion" is a very real thing. There are more and more people living in fewer and fewer regions, and they constitute an ever-changing pattern from the productive-dependent point of view.

There Is More Knowledge

Another characteristic of our times is the sheer increase in the amount of knowledge available in all fields. Increased expenditures for research and library procurement illustrate this generation of new knowledge in measurable form. Growth of abstracting services, information-retrieval systems, and specialized-knowledge systems dramatize the "explosion of knowledge" still more.

However one chooses to portray it, it is clear that the quantity and quality of information is developing steadily at what appears to be an accelerating pace. Part of the increase is a direct result of the population increase itself, but recent developments in communication, exploration, observation, and theorization are also responsible for this phenomenon.

Conflicting and Threatening Ideologies

Soviet Russia, China, and other Communist nations exist. Politically, we may choose not to recognize some of them, but they are realities nonetheless. These nations have adopted or devised economic, political, and social systems which are at variance with those systems which comprise what we call "the American way." The Russian Revolution occurred half a century ago, and more than a third of the world's population now functions under some modification of the Marxist-Leninist point of view. The fact that our people enjoy what we think is a "better life" does not negate the fact that Communist ideology and practice is an accomplished and accomplishing social scheme today.

Related to this conflict in ideology is the fact that man has developed his knowledge systems to the point that he is capable of complete and total destruction of the entire human race. That such annihilation will not occur is based at least as much on hope as on established fact. Although men have struggled for the past two decades to cope with this problem, both in the United Nations and at the Geneva Disarmament Talks, they have not been entirely successful. Some progress has been made, but until now there has been a trend toward a greater proliferation rather than elimination of destructive weaponry. "Overkill" is more than a cute military phrase. It represents a frightening situation in which man has more than enough destructive power necessary to completely obliterate his own world.

THE RESPONSE TO THE FORCES

None of these given conditions represents a particularly new development on the social scene. The American people have had more than twenty years in which to assess and make efforts to cope with even the most recent—the threat of thermonuclear war. Confronted with these forces, they have responded in various ways, often affecting the educational effort directly or indirectly. Four illustrative responses are described below: (1) the expansion of federal involvement, (2) the acceleration of social revolution, (3) the increased interest of the public in the school system, (4) the increase in the activities of extremists.

Expansion of Federal Involvement

The federal government has been active in educational affairs for more than a century. In response to incidents such as Sputnik, however, which symbolized the technological advance made by a Communist (and therefore threatening) nation, federal involvement in the field of education has expanded dramatically. The National Defense Education Act of 1958, for instance, encouraged schools to expend greater effort in the areas of mathematics, science, and foreign languages, especially. Guidance programs were also fostered with the implicit assumption that more youngsters would be guided into these supposedly imperative fields.

Increased allocation of funds for research and innovation in education were also initiated. Functioning through the National Science Foundation (NSF) and the United States Office of Education (USOE), major efforts at curriculum revision appeared in the form of such projects as the Physical Science Study Committee (PSSC Physics), the School Mathematics Study Group (SMSG Mathematics), the Biological Science Curriculum Study (BSCS Biology), Project English, and Project Social Studies. In addition, major centers for promoting educational innovation and change sprang up under the auspices of the USOE. "Project Talent," a longitudinal study of almost half a million American secondary school students, was also sponsored primarily by federal funds.

In all of these efforts, the national government has attempted to function as a catalytic agent primarily through the employment of federal funds. No school system was forced to participate in NDEA programs. No college or university was required to offer institutes for the training of PSSC physics teachers or foreign language teachers or to seek funds for educational demonstration or research. In every case, the laws were written so that educational organizations, themselves, initiated requests to become involved. In this way, the problem of federal control was scrupulously avoided.

Although there was no pressure exerted by any federal agency for educational groups to participate in these programs, still the government stipulated that certain standards be maintained. Government leaders would be irresponsible if they provided public funds with no assurance that the money would be used to foster better educational programs. Some educators assert that this *modus operandi* is tantamount to federal control, but they fail to see the distinction between a government which proclaims "You *must* participate!" and one which merely says "You may participate."

Many programs funded by the federal government have encouraged change in public education. The Elementary and Secondary Education Act of 1965 (ESEA) allocated more than a billion dollars for programs in five areas:

Title I — $1,060,082,973 for financial assistance to local educational agencies for the education of children of low-income families; Title II — $100,000,000 for school library resources, textbooks, and other instructional materials; Title III — $100,000,000 for supplementary educational centers and services; Title IV — $100,000,000 for educational research and training; Title V — $25,000,000 for grants to strengthen state departments of education.

As a result of this legislation, more than 22,000 individual projects were funded throughout the country—remarkable progress in a short span of time.

Regional laboratories have been established to promote innovations in strategically located areas throughout the country. Research and development centers are promoting fundamental research to foster better educational programs. Much educational research has been accomplished and the results already published. ERIC Centers (Educational Research Information Centers) give teachers and administrators the opportunity to obtain research materials at very economical costs.

The federal government has also extended its sphere of influence in education through research and demonstration programs sponsored by such agencies as the National Institutes of Health and the Departments of Agriculture, Defense, and Labor.

In retrospect, it would appear that this extending federal involvement was generally to broaden educational opportunities rather than to strengthen existing programs. However, one can hardly fail to be impressed with the fact that federal involvement has increased.

Acceleration of Social Revolution

Responding to these dynamic forces, a series of social revolutions have been appearing throughout America and, in fact, throughout the world. The struggle for equality by the Negro has finally achieved major proportions in both scope and degree. This struggle has taken the form of physical violence, as a brief glance at the riot statistics for the past four years shows:[1]

---
[1]"The Cities — What Next," *Time,* XC (August 11, 1967), 11. See also Otto Kerner, *et al., Report of the National Advisory Commission on Civil Disorders* (New York: Bantam Books, 1968), Chap. 2.

		DEAD	INJURED	ARRESTED
1964	8 cities	8	1,056	2,643
1965	Watts, Chicago	35	1,080	4,310
1966	18 areas	12	366	1,647
1967	31 cities	86	2,056	11,094

In addition, many aspects of the Negro's struggle for equality occurred in schools; segregation, both *de facto* and *de jure,* is a prime example. The "War on Poverty" is another case in point. Confronted with increasing rigidity in the social system, many racial, religious, economic, and age groups initiated a variety of activities designed to further their own unique objectives.

Many of these efforts have affected education. For example, unrest in Africa changed the social studies curriculum; unequal educational opportunities brought about redistricting, transportation of pupils across neighborhood lines, and new instructional materials; and atrocities against individual persons facilitated passage of dramatic civil rights legislation which profoundedly affected schools. The changing pattern of social relationships and the pace of these various changes can only be described as a social revolution of sorts.

Increased Public Interest in the School System

People are more genuinely interested in education today. They write letters to newspapers, discuss educational problems among themselves on the streets, vote on school levies, participate in PTA groups, read news stories about their schools, and stay involved in continuing dialogue with school-board members, teachers, administrators, legislators, pressure groups, and others involved in the educational system.

Over a period of time, this participation has indicated that the public holds both positive and negative attitudes towards American education. On the one hand, there is widespread belief in and support of public education in America. On the other hand, failing bond issues, inadequate legislative support, and the continuous criticism of public schools suggest fairly widespread dissatisfaction with what goes on in schools.

Some of this negative public reaction probably stems from the disproportionate representation of the people in their state legislatures. Education is primarily an activity of each individual state, and everything which occurs in any given "local" school level has either been mandated or allowed by the state government. Since many state legislatures do not reflect the sentiments of the urban population groups, the clamor of such city groups relative to educational services often go unheeded. And when the state government does not reflect the views of the majority of the people who want a strong state program for education, inferior or mediocre schools result. In most states, rural population has traditionally been "over-represented," although bills for reapportionment have been introduced in many state legislatures throughout the country. Undoubtedly, new legislation in this area would be a real boon to state government leaders who take seriously their responsibility for a high-quality educational system.

Likewise, there is also some reason to believe that schools bear a disproportionate amount of negative public response simply because they represent the one place where citizens can reach out and vote directly for or against the ideas proposed by the governmental unit involved. In the tradition of "local control," taxpayers often vote directly on the funds involved in educational expenditures. Only in rare instances, however, do these same taxpayers have an opportunity to cast ballots for expenditures designated for roads or prisons or the armed forces. Since many persons resent the growth of government of any kind, they strike back directly and vote "no" at any point they can.

Rise of the Extremists

Fear narrows one's perspective. This is a demonstrated psychological fact. Confronted with a threatening situation, the frightened person's perceptual field narrows. And many aspects of the social scene today are frightening. Communist expansion, the possibility of a nuclear war, and racial riots for example, have sharply narrowed many views of the educational enterprise. Sensing a "do or die" situation, frightened people have banded together in an effort to wage common war on "the bad group," whoever they might be.

The Necessity for Educational Change 9

Studies by Nelson,[2] Raywid,[3] and Commager,[4] demonstrate the impact that extremists, as critics, have made upon education. Educators typically have adopted a constricted posture in their efforts to avoid further criticism from such reactionary groups; they have often modified their procedures to fit within the critics' frame of reference. Thus, the extremists' point of view has frequently prevailed, even though public pronouncements or policy decisions generally appear to have taken another form. By adopting a "let's avoid criticism" stance, educators often allow themselves to be placed in the unfortunate position of securing the critics' demands even before they arrive on the scene. This phenomenon occurs because of a kind of "ripple effect" of the extremists' criticism of schools.

When the library offerings in one community are questioned by extremist groups, for example, librarians and administrators in surrounding areas quietly but hurriedly remove such volumes from their own library shelves. Even though the original school under fire may fight through their case to a satisfactory solution, the impact upon other schools in the general area is such that the critics' ends are achieved.

THE PROBLEM DEFINED

More children and more knowledge both come to rest in classrooms at one time. The social revolution going on in America today occurs in large part in schools, also. Added to these pressures are the pervasive factors of international communism and the threat of major nuclear war. Wells' statement that "history becomes more and more a race between education and catastrophe" has genuine meaning for all people today.[5]

The responses of individuals and groups to these and

---

[2] Jack Nelson and Gene Roberts, Jr., *The Censors and the Schools* (Boston: Little, Brown and Company, 1963).

[3] Mary Anne Raywid, *The Ax-Grinders: Critics of Our Public Schools* (New York: The Macmillan Company, 1965).

[4] Henry Steele Commager, *Freedom, Loyalty, Dissent* (New York: Oxford University Press, 1954).

[5] H. G. Wells, *The Outline of History.* (Garden City, N. Y.: Garden City Publishing Co., 1920, 1931). p. 1169.

other pressures indicate that thoughtful people are concerned about schools and school people and what they do.

Education is a social organization, and every organization reflects two basic needs: the need to maintain and the need to improve. Schools are no exception to this general rule.

Meeting the problem of more children and more knowledge forces educators to expend much of their professional energy simply maintaining the basic operation which is already underway. Procuring sites, constructing buildings, selecting textbooks, preparing teachers, meeting classes, giving tests, filling out forms—these and a hundred other activities are all designed primarily to help maintain the educational effort.

But the need to improve is reflected, too. Supervision, for instance, is designed to help teachers improve in what they do. Inservice education, teachers' institutes, research conferences, summer school, new instructional materials, different organizational schemes—all are designed to help the educational effort improve.

Given the urgencies and the pace of the times, the case for educational change is born. Change for the sake of change is not desirable, of course, but progress in a democracy develops out of the sensitive and intelligent use of information as a basis for rational change. That means two things: "good" data must be available, and the system must be organized and function in such a way that these data are utilized. Chapter Two will review our previous efforts to bring about significant educational change.

Chapter Two

Previous Efforts at Educational Change

INTRODUCTION

Recognizing the changing tenor of the times, educators have regularly worked to bring about meaningful and appropriate educational change. Some of the changes proposed were based on strict logic or on common sense; others were rooted in the authority of a particular man. Still other propositions for change were predicated upon empirical research data. Some drew their inspiration from tradition and the past.

Educators have not been lazy or negligent. Aware of their problem, these devoted and energetic men have advanced one proposition after another related to educational change. The purpose of this chapter is to review some of these efforts.

HYPOTHESES REGARDING EDUCATIONAL CHANGE

There are many ways in which one might organize a discussion of the varied approaches which have been attempted at educational change. Inasmuch as most of the innovations and modifications which were attempted in the past had not been proven when they first began, they will be described here as *hypotheses* regarding educational change. In almost every instance, educators were careful in evaluating each proposal's potential for desirable change, however the untested nature of most of our previous efforts makes the notion of "hypotheses" appropriate. And because certain change efforts involved similar domains, they have been grouped here into crude categories to facilitate an exploration of the ideas involved. These categories are neither discrete nor comprehensive, but simply illustrative and hopefully useful as constructs with which to think about educational change. They include efforts which involved modification of subject-matter content, organization, methods, leadership, research, and teacher personnel. Each of these groupings is discussed as encompassing a series of hypotheses relative to educational change.

Content Hypotheses

Over the years, additions, deletions, or modifications of what was being taught have been undertaken to bring about educational change. Franklin introduced the "practical" subjects of foreign language and trigonometry into the academy of his day to help young men who worked in the ports and went to sea. Eliott introduced the concept of educational electives by adding biology to the curriculum at Harvard after the general faculty had turned his request down to make it a part of the required program. Courses in vocational agriculture, home economics, and trade and industrial education became part of most American high schools after passage of the Smith-Lever Act in 1914 and the later Smith-Hughes Act of 1917. In every case, these changes in the educational effort were predicated upon fundamental changes in *what* was being taught; they involved subject-matter content.

In recent years, several groupings of content hypotheses have appeared under the sponsorship of various subject-matter groups. Physical Science Study Committee (PSSC) physics, School Mathematics Study Group (SMSG) mathe-

Previous Efforts at Educational Change

matics, Chemical Education Material Study (CHEM) and Chemical Bond Approach (CBA) chemistry programs, Biological Sciences Curriculum Study (BSCS) biology, Project English, Project Social Studies, and the Foreign Language Elementary School (FLES) program of foreign language instruction in the elementary school are all cases in point. Receiving their initial impetus from one or more of the academic disciplines involved, major curriculum revision programs such as these have proceeded on the assumption that by restructuring, relabeling, and reconceptualizing the basic ideas inherent in the discipline itself, fundamental changes in the educational operation would ensue. Recent developments in structural-linguistics and generative grammar have resulted in various curricular programs to incorporate these recent findings into experimental programs for public schools. Developments in terms of the DNA concept in modecular biology and the chemical-bond approach in chemistry have prompted revisionists in these fields to hypothesize new forms of content as appropriate for public schools. Rewriting curriculum guides and textbook selection procedures also constitute content change hypotheses.

Any careful look at American education over an extended period of time convinces one that educators have regularly attempted to improve the educational enterprise by advancing subject-matter content hypotheses to effect significant change.

Organizational Hypotheses

As a social institution, education is organized. Many of the hypotheses regarding educational change have traditionally focused upon modifications of the organizational aspects. For example, schooling typically involves groups of youngsters working together with one or more teachers over extended periods of time. It has been natural, therefore, that educators have attempted to bring about important educational change through manipulation of the various grouping variables which were involved: time, space, staff, and criteria for grouping, especially.

Major educational plans such as team teaching, the

middle school, the nongraded school, and the core program have all been educational changes which presupposed organizational change as a major theme. Grouping children by ability, achievement, age, sex, and previous experience involves the same kind of assumptions. School-district consolidation, large-group instruction, small-group discussion, independent study, and the 8-4, 6-3-3, 6-6, 4-4-4 kinds of organizational patterns all reflect interest in improving education by varying the organizational features in some particular way. Even the development of school study groups and curriculum councils have been instances of organizational hypotheses set forth to promote positive educational change. One can hardly fail to be impressed with the fact that educators have diligently sought to improve education by seeking new and different and hopefully better organizational schemes.

Methodological Hypotheses

Another category of hypotheses embraces efforts predicated primarily upon methodological change. Language laboratories, educational television, programmed instruction, (ITA) Initial Teaching Alphabet, teacher-pupil planning, and the project method are all illustrations of this kind of change. Employing discussion rather than lecture, laboratory work in addition to classroom practice, field study, introduction of phonics at an earlier age, film-strip projectors, the talking typewriter and other audio-visual aids, diagnostic testing, and even homework are examples of methodological variations employed in schools to foster appropriate educational gain. The unit method, interaction analysis, and computer-based teaching machines are still further examples.

Leadership Hypotheses

Drawing upon the research in human relations and group dynamics, educators have also fashioned a series of hypotheses to promote educational change designed to release the creative potential of all persons. Action research projects, inservice study groups, sensitivity training, and lay curriculum committees are all efforts to uncover and tap the latent abilities of people holding non-status positions, but who may make strong contributions to educational change. Recognizing the tremendous possibilities which typically lie dormant within almost every social group, educators have struggled to devise the ways of working and the atmosphere which would allow all of these potential ideas for educational change to come to the fore. Democratic group relations, involvement in decision-making, and meaningful participation have been recurring themes. A major shift from the traditional conceptions of authority to group interaction and process-type goals has been evident for several years.

Borrowing from the research in sociology, social psychology, business, and industry has been one characteristic of such leadership hypotheses. Another has been a growing awareness of the "if you do not do it democratically, you have to do it over" kind of practical consideration of educational change.

Research Hypotheses

Beginning about the turn of the century, interest in educational research began to grow. Excited by Thorndike and encouraged by Dewey, educators sought to bring the procedures and power of science to the educational domain. In the more than half-century since the original efforts, education has been steadily, if not remarkably, transformed. The latter third of this century promises even more educational research aimed at promoting significant educational change.

Descriptive studies by large school systems, the National Education Association, and the U. S. Office of Education have forced attention on such problems as retention in grade, dropouts, teacher turnover, and working conditions for teachers. Experimental studies of learning, forgetting, transfer, grouping, teaching methods, and instructional materials have generated useful data. Action research as an inservice tool has been predicated upon the prinicples of involvement and learning as well as research to encourage positive forms of educational change.

Spurred on by increased appropriations under the Cooperative Research Program of the United States Office of Education and the National Institute of Mental Health, for example, educators have expended greater and greater effort to research the problems in education in every imaginable way. Between 1964 and 1965, as an illustration, the appropriation of funds for educational research in the USOE alone increased fourfold. Using areas such as agriculture or medicine as models, educators have attempted to formulate new conceptions of the process of educational change. For example, bridging the distance from basic research in botany to the farmer in the field has brought about developments in agriculture designed to serve as communication links in the overall bridge. Between the botanist and farmer, therefore, the university researcher (e.g., an agronomist), the agricultural experimental station, and the county agent have been brought together to expedite and implement agricultural change. Even though the botanist and the farmer are widely separated in time and space and in more fundamental psychological ways, the basic assumption seems to be that intervening persons can "carry the message" and expand the implications in practical terms so that new concepts and new data in the agricultural field can find their way into farming practice. The research-development, R-D bridge has been buttressed with functional pillars in the form of specialized agencies and men who facilitate and communicate from the researcher to the development phase and from the developmental activities back to the researcher. This two-way communication enables the operation to function effectively.

Personnel Hypotheses

Teachers are obviously important elements in the educational endeavor. Realizing this, many efforts to promote educational change have focused upon the personnel involved. In some cases, these hypotheses have been built around the idea of basic changes in teacher-education programs. In still other approaches, the concepts of supervision and inservice education, especially, have leveled their efforts at remaking and improving teachers already on the job.

Previous Efforts at Educational Change

Many of the activities of teacher-training institutions in the past twenty years have come forth as "Fifth-Year" programs, "Master of Arts in Teaching" programs, and revised undergraduate programs involving increased laboratory experiences with children, internship in place of practice teaching, subject-matter "majors" for prospective elementary teachers, and the like. Encouraged by foundations, especially, universities and colleges have attempted various programmatic schemes to help the liberal arts graduate untrained for teaching make a successful transit into the school system.

In an entirely different vein, Lieberman,[1,2,3] Stinnett,[4,5,6,7] and others have focused attention on the concept of professionalism and professional negotiations as a means to a better educational end. The growing antagonism between the American Federation of Teachers and the National Education Association is further evidence of the professionalism trend. Sanctions, strikes, certification, and self-discipline all relate to educators' activities designed to improve both the caliber and number of persons who work with youth in schools.

THE TESTING OF THESE HYPOTHESES

The major themes which we have considered thus far are two: (1) there has been and still is a need for educa-

---

[1] Myron Lieberman and Michael H. Moskow, *Collective Negotiations for Teachers: An Approach to School Administration* (Chicago: Rand McNally & Company, 1966).

[2] Myron Lieberman, *Education as a Profession* (Englewood Cliffs, N.J.: Prentice-Hall, Inc., 1956).

[3] Myron Lieberman, *The Future of Public Education* (Chicago: University of Chicago Press, 1960).

[4] Timothy M. Stinnett, *The Profession of Teaching* (Washington, D.C.: Center for Applied Research in Education, 1962).

[5] Timothy M. Stinnett and G. K. Kleinman, *The Education of Teachers: Conflict and Consensus* (Englewood Cliffs, N.J.: Prentice-Hall, Inc., 1961).

[6] Timothy M. Stinnett and Albert J. Huggett, *Professional Problems of Teachers* (New York: The Macmillan Company, 1956, 1963).

[7] Timothy M. Stinnett, *Professional Negotiation in Public Education* (New York: The Macmillan Company, 1966).

tional change, and (2) there have been many change efforts described here as hypotheses. But what have been the results of these efforts? Two conclusions seem evident: much change has occurred, but, in general, this change has not been significant in an educational sense. In the sections which follow, the data pertaining to these two generalizations will be briefly described, including a summary explanation of how this predicament apparently arose.

Evidence of Educational Change

Even a cursory view of schools today compared to those of twenty years ago suggests that there has been a considerable change in the field of education.

First of all, school buildings have changed. They are bigger, lighter, more colorful, and have more varied facilities and equipment than schools ever had before. Greenboards, carpeting, air conditioning, cafeterias, television receivers, movable walls, and intraschool communication equipment are modern innovations.

In terms of program, there have been many changes, too. Curriculum offerings are both broader and deeper. More courses in mathematics, science, foreign language, literature, industrial arts, vocational education, and physical education are evident. The concepts of "team teaching" and "programmed instruction" are not especially new, but the extent to which they permeate education are much greater than ever before. Cawelti's discussion of these concepts in American high schools in the mid-1960's provides one excellent overview.[8]

It has been estimated that more than fifty per cent of the high school students studying physics in the United States today are involved in PSSC physics programs, thousands are utilizing the BSCS programs in biology, and an estimated hundreds of thousands of students from elementary school through college participate in programs employing educational television. And none of these programs existed before 1950.

---

[8]Gordon Cawelti, "Innovative Practices in High Schools: Who Does What- and Why-and How," *Nation's Schools*, LXXIX (April, 1967), 56-90 passim.

The Question of Significance

Granting that these many changes have occurred, have they made any difference? Were the changes significant in any way?

"Significance" can be determined statistically, logically, philosophically, or in other ways. In general terms, this writer presumes that any change is significant if it makes an *important difference* in the lives and minds of the students involved. Two specific criteria inhere in this concept of significance. First, the difference will manifest itself in the lives of those students being served. Second, something about the difference will indicate that it has sufficient impact to be considered important. This is a very subjective factor, to be sure. If the change results in considerable or crucial differences in the behavior of those who experience the change, it is assumed to be significant. It should also be pointed out, however, that the significance of any educational change has direction as well as intensity. It can be either positive or negative. No one ever hopes for or deliberately works toward negative changes in education, but they do occur. The discussion below may clarify these points to some degree.

One of the most interesting but disturbing observations one can make regarding most of the newer programs is that there is almost no research being done to determine whether or not they are satisfactory. There are, of course, exceptions to this generalization. Research in the area of educational television and programmed instruction, for example, has been extensive. But one looks in vain for studies comparing the effectiveness of PSSC Physics or SMSG Mathematics or team teaching or language laboratories with other approaches in these fields. There are very few. And the studies which have been done usually suggest that there are no significant differences in the several programs involved.[9] One can only conclude that many of the hypotheses for educational change have failed.

---

[9]Appendix A lists some of the research upon which these conclusions are based.

WHY THESE HYPOTHESES HAVE FAILED

First of all, many persons will reject the interpretation that these hypotheses have failed. They will maintain that the programs are too new to be evaluated or that it is not reasonable to compare the newer programs with conventional ones because their purposes vary. They may even suggest that this writer is opposed to educational change. These are all legitimate viewpoints which deserve attention. This writer believes that many of existing practices and programs in education are inappropriate and must be changed. He also believes that many of the newer ventures are soundly based. The learning principles upon which they are built are generally defensible and clear, the effort to update content and methodology is admirable, and the cooperation of scholars and practicing educators is a very encouraging sign. Nonetheless, it seems evident that most of the efforts to date have failed or are failing now. At least four suggestions could be given for these failures: (1) we have asked the wrong questions, (2) we have manipulated the wrong variables, (3) we have made the wrong assumptions, and (4) the total system has a fundamental flaw. The remaining portion of this chapter will be devoted to a brief consideration of the first three points. The following chapter will explore the problem posed in point four.

We Ask the Wrong Questions

Confronted with the possibility of making a decision or interpretation regarding educational change, we sometimes ask such questions as, "How many schools are using PSSC physics this year?" or "How many children are involved in closed circuit ETV?" or "How many teachers are using ITA?" These are *frequency questions;* if we ask a frequency question, we always get a frequency answer. For example:

Q. "How many schools use the PSSC physics program?

A. "About fifty per cent of the American high schools teach PSSC physics at the present time."

These are interesting data, to be sure. But suppose that we do know that approximately fifty per cent of the high schools now teaching physics are using the PSSC physics program. Does the widespread existence or extensive participation in a program suggest a significant educational change?

To some people, the answer to this question is generally "Yes." There is the subtle implication that "if so many schools are using it, it must be good." The gentle shifting from frequency to desirability is prevalent in education. Sometimes recognized as the "bandwagon" approach to curriculum change, few persons advocate but many appear to follow such logic in their operations day by day.

It is not uncommon, for example, for superintendents or curriculum directors to urge adoption of some new program "because most of the best schools have it." The unstated assumption, of course, is that "the other schools must have examined the program carefully before they tried it, so why should we?"

Examined carefully, such an argument has little merit. No one would suggest that such practices as crime, prostitution, or discrimination ought to be adopted by society at large, even though they exist in fairly widespread form. It is often felt in education, however, that if we get positive answers to the frequency question, then we ought to move in those directions in terms of educational change. Let's return to the PSSC physics example which was cited before.

True, almost fifty per cent of American high schools do teach PSSC physics today, but the proportion of high school students taking physics has dropped eighteen per cent since the program began.[10] The PSSC physics program may be an outstanding example of desirable educational change, but one cannot help but wonder why the proportional enrollment has steadily declined since the program began. Whether the decrease has occurred in PSSC physics or non-PSSC physics schools is not known as of now. Such factors as increased pressure for college acceptance may have caused some students to avoid high school physics courses as a means of improving their rank in class, but

---
[10]Computed from data reported by John Walsh in "Curriculum Reform," *Science*, CXLIV (May 8, 1964), 642-646.

the fact remains that sheer increase in the number of schools using PSSC physics programs is absolutely no clue as to the appropriateness or desirability of such programs in effecting educational change. Considering the fact that the newer program supposedly causes students to "want to learn physics," the proportional decrease in student enrollment must be considered at least as important as the extensiveness of the program in schools across the land.

The frequency question is simply the wrong question to ask. But we have other kinds of questions that also miss the point.

"Does the teacher have a right to whip a child?" This is a *legal question*, obviously. "Can superintendents direct teachers to remove certain books from reading lists?" "Do principals have an authority to tell teachers how to teach?" These are also questions that are basically legal in nature.

"Will we be getting our money's worth?" "How much will it cost?" "Is it efficient?" These are *economic questions*, in the main.

Education has a legal side, of course, and the financial base is an important secondary consideration, too. But even the laws are not always right. Even more important, though, legal questions and economic questions have a way of forcing themselves to the foreground of discussion and overriding consideration of the more important effectiveness problem unless educators are wary.

If a proposed educational change will cost more than the existing program, questions of an economical nature arise. If the change is better in effectiveness terms, then the unpleasant question which emerges is, "Is the basic purpose of the schools to save money or to help children learn?" If the basic purpose is to save taxpayers' funds, then many modifications of program could undoubtedly be made. On the other hand, if the basic purpose is to help children learn, then the financial considerations are not the fundamental but rather a secondary problem which is involved.

The questions that are meaningful are the *effectiveness questions*. "Is it effective?" "Will it make a significant difference in the lives of those students who will be involved?" "Will they learn more, better, faster?" "Will they be changed in important and desirable ways?"

The effectiveness question must always dominate the scene when considering educational change. Whether the new effort is widely adopted or not at all, whether it is legal or illegal, or expensive or inexpensive are not fundamental problems. The question is, "Does it help us to realize our educational objectives more fully or in less time or more lastingly than any other way?"

The point is, if we ask the wrong questions, we will always get inadequate answers. Thoughtful educators concerned with promoting positive educational change must be cognizant of the educational trends and the costs and the legal dimensions which are involved. But they must always press their questions in effectiveness terms. One of the reasons we have not been very successful is that we have asked many wrong questions of ourselves again and again.

We Manipulate the Wrong Variables

Anyone who has read the research on grouping, methods of teaching reading, educational television, or on any of a host of problem areas in education generally concludes two things: (1) the pattern of results generally shows that "no significant difference" is actually involved, and (2) the teacher is probably the most crucial variable in the educational effort.

What seems to have occurred over the years is that educators have unwittingly fallen into the trap of trying to manipulate the external variables "out there," apart from the teacher: class size, criteria for grouping, presentation techniques, and the like. Everybody knows, intuitively as well as from the research that has been done, that teachers are by far the most important variable in the learning situation. Given the alternative of effecting significant change through varying class size or varying the teaching personnel, everything that we know now would suggest that far greater changes would accrue if we could change the people who are involved. But the idea of "changing people" literally or psychologically carries with it the assumption that the present people are less than perfect or that they are inadequate in some important way.

Many educators are reluctant to admit, even to themselves, that their "teaching personality" or their classroom performance is less than satisfactory. So they deny the idea altogether, and the result is a vicious circle. Educators know intuitively or otherwise that if they hope for significant change, they must change themselves. Yet, the threatening aspect of such an idea forces them to look elsewhere for other variables to manipulate; therefore, they become one more step removed from the crux of the problem — better teachers and better teaching performance.

We Make the Wrong Assumptions

Clearly tied to the fact that we tend to ask the wrong questions and manipulate the wrong variables is the idea that we make the wrong assumptions. Perhaps an illustration will make this point more clear.

Under our present ways of working, those of us who seek to foster improvement in education in effect say to the teachers involved:

> Here is a new idea. Try it out. Work hard. Learn all of the new factors and skills and knowledge which are involved. If you really try and really put yourself into it, children will learn more at the end of the year, and you will feel good about it.

For all practical purposes, we assume that altruism is an adequate motivational base from which to encourage teachers to adopt or incorporate important educational change into what or how they teach each day. But is this assumption reasonable? That is, is it reasonable to suppose that teachers can be encouraged to incorporate important kinds of educational change into their own teaching repertoire if all that we can promise them at the end of the year is a good feeling if improvement occurs?

Altruism is a powerful motivational force, that much is sure. However, in the business of working to foster widespread and significant educational change, is the promise of "a good feeling" and "an increase in satisfaction" from helping others enough to insure adoption of the new techniques or materials?

No other group in our society presupposes such a complete dependence upon altruism as a basis for change. If the farmer tries a new fertilizer and grows more bushels of corn per acre, he obtains a financial gain. If the physician or attorney is more successful, his practice improves and his income goes up. If the private in the Army does a better job, he can hope to be promoted and reap a monetary gain. Even ministers who do a better job end up with bigger churches and larger salaries. With the exception of Catholic priests and nuns who take the vow of poverty, almost no one in our society is expected to do an ever-better job on the assumption that an increase in satisfaction from helping others will suffice to encourage them to change. No one except public school teachers, that is.

It would appear that the concept of "merit pay" is somehow related to educational change. In a society permeated with materialistic concerns, a complete dependence upon altruism ought to be questioned, at least.

Other assumptions in the educational effort need to be questioned, too: grade level as a basis for organizing schools to help children learn; grading as a basis for encouraging youngsters to achieve; and "temporary certificates" for teachers who are obviously not qualified, to cite a few. Education is shot through with untested assumptions which are now rooted in tradition and are therefore difficult to change. Each of these assumptions should be subjected to empirical and logical scrutiny.

SUMMARY

These are very difficult and trying times. Faced with both the prospect and need for significant change, educators have advanced several different kinds of hypotheses designed to bring it about. They have worked to change the content, the organizational patterns in schools, the methodology involved, the leadership activities, the research, and the human element, too. In general, these efforts have been less than successful. Some of the reasons probably stem from the fact that we have traditionally posed the wrong kinds of questions, we have manipulated the wrong variables, and we have made erroneous assumptions regarding what would foster important change. A very basic question still remains, however. Conceptually regarded, is education capable of change? The chapter which follows will take up this problem and treat education as a social system.

Chapter Three

The Social Systems Concept and Education

INTRODUCTION

Education is a social system. Conceptually, it embraces diverse groups bound together in working relationships to further particular ends. The purpose of this chapter is to explore the idea of a social system and to examine various attributes of different social systems as they are in evidence today.

THE SOCIAL SYSTEMS CONCEPT

As used throughout this book, a social system represents a human undertaking aimed at furthering some particular human cause. Government is a social system. Religion, medicine, industrial production, and science can also be viewed as social systems. Every social system, large or small, involves a number of people working together in unique but cooperative ways to realize the attainment of some social end. Viewed in this way, education is unquestionably a social system.

Social systems have certain common elements, but they also differ in some respects. Purposes give direction to all social systems, but purposes vary both broadly and in detail. Medicine aims to help men live a longer, healthier, less painful life. Religion attempts to help each man establish a meaningful relationship between himself and his God. Business and industry work to produce particular services or goods and thus create capital and personal gain. Science seeks to describe and predict the multitudinous facets of the natural world. Every social system has a specific purpose or basic intention which it strives to realize or fulfill. Purposes vary but purposes are always present.

Social systems also vary in terms of the procedures or means which they employ. The operations of an industrial system are not the same as those of a scientific, religious, or educational system. Every social system, though, seeks to attain its avowed purposes in particular ways.

Social systems also differ in terms of the way the effectiveness of the total system is determined. Assessing the operation of each system occurs in a multitude of ways. An industrial concern either makes money or loses it; there is no in-between. The hypothesis in science is upheld or disproved. And children either learn or they fail to learn when we teach in school. Evaluation always reflects degrees as well as direction, however, and no simple "either-or" categorization is intended here. The main point is that every social system attempts to evaluate the effectiveness of the ongoing system.

Stated another way, every social system has three basic aspects or parts of the overall system. One aspect involves the planning phase of the system, another aspect involves the doing phase, and a final aspect involves the evaluation phase. Each phase is interrelated with the others in dynamic yet balanced ways which, taken together, constitute a kind of recurring cycle or conceptual spiral in both time and space. In this sense, each phase feeds back into the whole; there is no real beginning or end to the system at all. For purposes of this discussion, however, a linear approach will be employed in considering each phase. We will simply try to "hold the system still" and look at a dynamic system in a fairly static way.

The Planning Phase

Every social system begins operating at the planning phase. It is here that the big ideas, the dreams, the policies, and the hypotheses are first articulated. Regardless of the precise manifestations, each social system begins its efforts with a theorizing approach.

In government, for example, laws are made. Congress or the state legislature or the city council sits down, plans, and thinks. The members hypothesize, so to speak, that the particular conditions they will decree will be appropriate to solve whatever human problems brought them together or engaged their attention. Finally, they act in legislative ways. They pass laws. They adopt ordinances.

In industry, the board of directors considers the available data and then adopts certain policies or sets certain directions. The basic purpose of the board members is to realize the ultimate aim of the particular corporation which is involved. The most obvious characteristic of their approach to the task includes decision-making about the direction in which the company should go, what kinds of products it should attempt to make, and what plans are appropriate for the maintenance and improvement of the company. This is the planning phase.

The Doing Phase

Once ideas are born and plans are made, once laws are passed and policies prepared and hypotheses stated, the second phase of the system comes into view. This is the doing phase. Laws must be executed. Hypotheses must be tested and rejected or verified. Plans must be translated into realities.

As far as government is concerned, the executive branch fulfills this phase in the American system. The President enforces the law. Governors enforce and execute the law. Mayors conduct their offices in a similar manner. Under their direction, the various branches of the executive arm of the government see to it that the plans laid down by the legislative group are faithfully carried through. Their task is not to make the law but to see that the law is realistically and appropriately applied.

In industry, management and workers combine to effect the policies and plans set forth by the board of directors. They function in ways entirely different from the executive branch of the government, but the doing phase of both systems still works to implement the ideas of the planning phase. And every social system is the same.

In the process of science, the experiment is conducted and, in this way, the hypothesis originally conceived is actually tried.

The Evaluating Phase

After policies have been made and implemented, the evaluative phase of the system comes into play. Products are judged, services guaged, laws interpreted, and inferences made. The assessment phase of any social system is accomplished in a variety of ways, but evaluation takes place in every case.

In government, after the legislature has passed a law and the executive branch of the government has enforced the law, the judicial group makes judgments pertaining both to the law itself and to the manner in which the enforcement was carried through. Because our system is predicated upon a government of laws and not of men, these interpretations are publicized and codified and exert an impact back upon both of the other two processes.

In industry, the evaluative phase takes an entirely different form. The product first goes into the market place. The buying public then looks at the product, sizes it up and tries it out. Under our free enterprise system, this is how evaluations are made. The buyer expresses his judgment—his evaluation—either by purchasing the product or shaking his head and walking away.

In science, the data produced in the experiment are considered and weighed, and evaluations of the hypothesis occur. Either the hypothesis is accepted or rejected or modified in some manner. Judgments and inferences are always made. *The Integrity of Science: A Report by the AASA Committee in Science in the Promotion of Human Welfare* provides some valuable insight into the working of a self-corrective system:

Free dissemination of information and open discussion is an essential part of the scientific process. Each separate study of nature yields an approximate result and inevitably contains some errors and omissions. Science gets at the truth by a continuous process of self-examination which remedies omissions and corrects errors. This process requires free disclosure of results, general dissemination of findings, interpretations, conclusions, and widespread verification and criticism of results and conclusions.[1]

In college football, the referee and his fellow officials make judgments as to whether the rules set forth by the NCAA are faithfully adhered to by the coaches and players in their execution of the game. If the play falls within the specific framework of the rules of the game, it is allowed to proceed with a minimum of interference from the officials. On the other hand, if the officials believe that there is a deviation from the rules, then by means of whistle and flag they bring the game to a halt and make interpretations and judgments which change the course of the game.

THE POWER OF THE SYSTEMS CONCEPT

Describing social systems in operation might be nothing more than an academic exercise were it not for one important point: each social system which has been described reflects an inherent power to improve itself and to manifest significant social change.

In effect, this power to improve and change inheres in the evaluative phase. It is no accident that science as a human process for solving problems is more productive and more effective than any other problem-solving method. It is no accident that the free enterprise economic system in America has outproduced every other kind of economic system ever known to man. The American people enjoy the benefits of social systems which are both dynamic and stable, but still responsive to the human needs of the day. The qualities of responsiveness and stability and dynamic change all flow from the fact that these social systems

---
[1] *American Scientist*, LIII (June, 1965), preprint.

are able to profit and grow from the evaluative process inherent in them. Evaluative feedback is the element which allows change to occur.

But the kind of change evident in the systems described thus far is more than "allowed" to occur; it is *made* to occur. There is an insistence from within the system itself that necessary changes take place. And these changes most often occur in a *reasonable* way.

Change Must Occur

When the buying public refuses to purchase a particular commodity or service, change occurs. When the referee blows his whistle, change occurs. When the court rules that a particular piece of legislation is unconstitutional and therefore invalid, change occurs.

Assume for a moment the eventualities which would take place if an automobile manufacturer continued to produce cars that no one would buy. Sooner or later that corporation would reach a point of industrial suicide; bankruptcy is the term we generally employ. Because resources are not without limit, those who make the policy and those who carry it through in the industrial world *have to pay attention to feedback.* This feedback comes from the buyers, who have both a mind and a power all their own in the judgment-making phase of the operation involved.

The same is true with the officials on the football field or with the courts. When the referee blows his whistle and throws his flag, he says, in effect, to the ball player who has breached the rules of the game, "Sonny, you can't do that, you know." And the ball player recognizes his authority. When the courts say, "That law is invalid because it violates the constitution," both the legislative and the executive branches of the government pay attention to the feedback.

Feedback Is Corrective

When a prospective buyer makes his judgment known in terms of a purchase or his refusal to buy, what he really does is force back into the system new data which assume a corrective role. The real power of the free enterprise system, in fact, lies not in competition, as is generally supposed, but in the free will of the consumer to make decisions regarding what he will and will not buy. Producers compete for the buyer's attention and dollar, to be sure, and in the process they seek to improve their product, but the real power of our economic system resides in the evaluations of the consumer rather than in the competition between producers.

And when the courts declare a particular law valid or invalid, what they really do is funnel new information back into the system which enables the system to improve. Over a period of time, because laws are codified and because every legal decision refers to a precise problem in both time and space, our governmental operation moves forward. Certain frailties and flaws may be evident, but the ability of the system to be responsive to extreme stresses and strains (e.g., assassinations of political leaders or the Negro social reform demands) reflects both a stability and capacity for significant change.

A picture of science processing new information has been beautifully portrayed by the American Association for the Advancement of Science Committee on Science in the Promotion of Human Welfare:

> A scientist can obscure the truth about a scientific question only by keeping silent about what he knows, or believes he knows, or by otherwise obstructing the publication of scientific results. Erroneous statements, so long as they are openly published, do not indefinitely impede the progress of science for they are ultimately corrected by new observations and interpretations. If scientists adhere to the rule of open publication of results, interpretations, and theoretical derivations, *nothing that they do can prevent the operation of the self-corrective processes of science.* It is this very process of claim and counterclaim which accomplishes the gradual progress toward truth in science.[2]

Even if scientists lie about what they know or think they know, the process of science will force the truth out. Only if pertinent information is withheld can the falsehood or

---

[2] Barry Commoner, *et al.* "Science and the Race Problem," *Science*, CXLII (November 1, 1963), 559. See also "Science and Human Survival," *Science*, CXXIV (December 29, 1961), 2080-2083.

error prevail. Because science is built upon the idea that separate persons can view the same phenomena in similar ways, reporting what they see, the system of science is able to prosper and grow from the scientific criticism which is assured.

In America, the First Amendment to the Constitution of the United States guarantees every citizen freedom of speech and press. In this way, our nation is provided with the opportunity to benefit from criticism of any kind. Democracy thrives on dissent and disagreement. This is freedom's self-corrective way.

Change Is Orderly

Brutal dictatorships and benevolent despots can both bring about social change. Over an extended period of time, however, autocratic change is bound to fail because the powers that be are unable to foresee the myriad eventualities which cause most changes to go astray. Not having the benefits of precise, corrective feedback, traumatic revolutions or ineffective changes are generally the order of the day under the autocratic system.

In a democracy or in science or in an economic system based on free enterprise, however, change is generally orderly and reasonable. This is the result of several unique factors.

It has been already mentioned that evaluative groups have power—they are independent—in the various systems described thus far. But that point is only partly true. Even though the courts or referees or buying public have independent power, they are dependent upon the policy-makers and producers, too. In government, this dependence is reflected partially in our system of checks and balances (e.g., the President appoints persons to the Supreme Court but the Senate must concur; Congress passes laws but the President must approve), but also in unstated assumptions that relationships involving give and take are actually the most effective way. Congress alone legislates our national law, but over the years this body has been generally receptive to proposals from the President regarding the need for legislative change. And where courts have declared certain legislation illegal, they have always been dependent

The Social Systems Concept and Education 35

upon the executive branches to see to it that their interpretations are in fact imposed. The courts have no enforcement power of their own. In this way, a very balanced, poised, dynamic system has been formed.

Like the homeostatic mechanisms, which keep all of the chemical changes fluctuating in positive, health-producing ways within the body, governmental, scientific, and industrial production systems in our nation maintain a continuous effort to balance the forces of interdependence and independence, autonomy and power, and separation and integration so that orderly progress and change will take place. The concept of federalism in government is another illustration of this point, too.

The results are obvious. This nation has an enviable record of orderly progress and development since the first thirteen states were formed. With one major exception (i.e., The Civil War), development and growth of the country has generally been rational and sustained.

In the area of economics, the same situation is also true. Over the years, there have been both major and minor ups and downs, but free enterprise and the republican-type governmental system have been flexible enough to outproduce every other country in the world. And the economic operation in America today bears little resemblance in form or theory to what it was when our nation was founded. Many of the changes have been radical, but none were forced by revolution or dictatorial control.

THE INADEQUACY IN THE EDUCATIONAL SYSTEM

At the beginning of this chapter, it is stated that education is a social system. The preceding analysis, however, deliberately avoids a consideration of the particulars of education as a system. This is because the educational system seems to have a fundamental flaw. This basic defect is described below.

The Educational System Is Incomplete

Conceptually, education as a social system is missing a vital element. One group makes educational policy, another group carries that policy through—but there is no formal or informally constituted group to judge the effectiveness of the system at all. The evaluating phase of the educational system is simply a void, although some persons will argue that this is not true.

If we ask the question, "Is there a group which makes policies, plans, and hypotheses about the direction in which education should go?" the answer is clearly "Yes." In our society, education is a function of the various states, and in each state constitutional or statutory legislation has created school boards for each school district and has directed those boards to play the policy-making role. The educational system is a part of the larger governmental system, to be sure, but within the educational-system concept there is one segment of the system which fulfills the thinking, planning, policy-making phase.

There is also a group which attends to the doing or effecting phase. The professionals—teachers, administrators, supervisors, counselors, and the like—have as their major responsibility the carrying out of the educational policies which school boards and state legislatures propose. In their regular professional role of selecting content, organizing instruction, and utilizing particular methods to realize the policy-stated aims, teachers and others strive to accomplish the doing phase.

To this point, education as a social system corresponds quite closely to the other social systems which have been described. However, within the educational system, there is no separate group with power which seeks to assess the effectiveness of the total operation. There is no body called the "educational court" or the "educational referee" or the "educational buying public" which exercises influence through corrective feedback to make the system improve and change. The result is stagnation, confusion, and chaotic efforts all rolled up into one.

How Is Educational Evaluation Accomplished?

Who assesses the effectiveness of the educational operation? How are evaluations made? What criteria are considered as bench marks to measure against? In what manner and form do evaluations appear? How are evaluative data utilized? What consequences follow evaluations of any aspect of the educational scene? These questions warrant very careful study.

The major thesis of this book is that evaluations do not occur in such a way and by such a group that they influence education in positive and creative ways. When judgments about the educational effort do take place, they are typically sporadic and employ questionable criteria. The feedback data are seldom utilized. Let us consider some hypothetical illustrations as a means of assessing the problem.

A superintendent answers the telephone and a critic complains, "Why does Mrs. Jones have that filthy book, *Catcher in the Rye,* on my son's reading list in English class?" If the superintendent gets three or four more such calls, the odds are great that he will call in his assistant superintendent or the high school principal on the phone and tell him to look into the matter and report back to him, or to get the book off the reading list. On the surface, it would appear that the general public is playing an effective evaluative role here.

In another system, a school levy is proposed to the voters, but they vote it down on election day. Evaluation must be occurring here.

In still another system, the curriculum council has been conducting extensive studies of the effect of homogeneous vs. heterogeneous grouping practices upon junior high school students' achievements as measured by teachers' grades and standardized achievement scores. This research seems to be evaluation in a very careful way.

There is a fallacy in assuming that these judgments function to help the system improve, however. In both the first and last examples cited, there is absolutely no assurance that the feedback will be considered. Indeed, in the first example of the parent complaining about a particular book on her child's reading list, there is real reason to wonder whether the superintendent actually should do anything at all. In the case of the levy failure, on the other hand, a judgment is made known, but not infrequently in cases of this kind everybody involved says "Why?" or "What went wrong?" and "What made people unhappy, anyway?" The feedback lacks precision and is not necessarily corrective.

At present, education as a social system functions in such a manner that evaluative data either appear in an unusable form or the circumstances are such that those who are responsible for the operation *may* pay attention to the data or not, depending upon the pressures or politics involved. Seldom are the issues on a bond election clarified to the point that all know for certain what a particular kind of expression by the voting public actually means. Or, given clear data regarding any innovation or change, there is absolutely nothing in the system which says that in the light of the data "you *must* do thus and so." The fact is, the system as presently conceived is generally either too sensitive or not sensitive enough to the kinds of evaluative data which come its way.

Consider another illustration. Suppose a college student enrolled at a university with the avowed intention of becoming a teacher. Suppose, further, that as a part of his stipulated program in professional education he was required to take a course in Education 101, "Introduction to Teaching," and that this course contained 350 students in a large lecture session. Imagine that this student, during the course of a semester, said to himself, "Why do I have to take this course? I'm not learning anything worthwhile here. I think I'll try to find out why I have to sit through these boring lectures in this large group day after day."

What would happen if such a student went to his advisor and said, "Why do I have to take Education 101?" The odds are very great that the conversation would go something like this:

> Student: "Why do I have to take Education 101?"
> Advisor: "Don't you want to be a teacher?"
> Student: "Yes, but why do I have to take that course? There are so many students in the room, and I am so far away, I never really seem to get much from what goes on. What good will it do me?"

At this point in the discussion, the advisor might move in any one of several directions. He might choose to be supportive and listen to the student's complaint with a sympathetic ear. He might become directive and tell the student to try harder or go have a chat with the course instructor. Or he might encourage the student to consider a change of majors. "Maybe teaching really isn't for you," he might say. Whatever his next step, *the probability is very great that the advisor would presuppose the validity of the course as an essential requirement to help this student learn to become an effective teacher.*

In effect, this advisor would be postulating the necessity of this course requirement as a means of insuring that the prospective teacher would learn to think and feel and act in appropriate ways. This is how most university programs operate. The men who devise them never have to prove, even to themselves, that any particular course or experience does, in fact, make a significant difference in the lives and minds of those who are required to take the course. In other words, *the system presupposes the validity and appropriateness and worthwhileness of any curricular experience.* Nobody has to prove anything to anyone.

What would happen if, for one reason or another, universities or college professors had to prove that what they were doing in their courses did make a difference in the direction desired? What would happen if university people attempted to prove to themselves that any given course or field trip or laboratory experience or sequence of courses caused their students to be different, better kinds of people than they were before?

Such a conception is unheard of, for the most part, at the present time. This idea is not meant to imply that university programs are not worthwhile or effective, but it does suggest that effective programs are so because the logic or experience upon which they are based happens to be appropriate and correct, or else because they have devised some evaluative procedures of their own. Many programs, however, are not similarly blessed. Is it any wonder that studies like those of Jacob[3] and Remmers[4] point out that education often does not make the kind of difference for which we all hope. The fact of the matter is that education is presently built upon untested postulates rather

---

[3] Philip Jacob, *Changing Values in College* (New York: Harper and Brothers, 1957).

[4] H. H. Remmers, *Anti-Democratic Attitudes in American Schools* (Evanston, Ill.: Northwestern University Press, 1963).

than testable hypotheses. And they are postulates rather than hypotheses simply because *there is nothing in the system which demands that the process be submitted to any kind of external test.*

In effect, what we have in education today is a system in which the planning, doing, and evaluative roles are blurred. Everybody recognizes the need for assessing the effectiveness of the operation, so school boards appoint lay advisory committees, school administrators conduct extensive studies with their own professional staff, and college professors solicit student evaluations of the courses they teach. *But there is nothing in the system which requires that the evaluative data obtained must be utilized.* Advisory committees, for example, are just that—advisory. If the research data regarding the effectiveness of some particular effort comes out contrary to any "expert's" suggestion or tradition or local pressure group's wishes, the odds are very great that recommendations from the curriculum council or educational researchers will lie on the shelf. And if the student evaluations do not tell the professor what he wants to hear, he may throw them all in the wastebasket with an epithet and never ask for student evaluations again. In the "best" school systems and the "best" universities, the "best" educational leaders are those who consistently evaluate what they are doing in a systematic and comprehensive way, then pay attention to the evaluative feedback which they procure. But not all school systems are the "best."

The real crux of the educational problem lies in the fact that the same people who are responsible for planning policy or effecting plans also assume the evaluative role: the system is completely closed. It is authoritarian, by definition. When one person or a group of persons decides what should be done, carries the plans through, and then evaluates how well the job has been done, we call this a closed system, a dictatorship, or some such similar term. What would our country be like today if Congress had the power to pass judgment on the validity and constitutionality of the laws which it made? How effective would our economic system be if the policy makers or management and workers were free to ignore the buying public's decisions regarding consumer goods?

The real power of our governmental system and our economic system resides in the fact that the evaluative groups exist separately and function independently of the planning and doing groups. And when the evaluative judgments are made, the planning and doing groups pay attention to the decisions which are made on the basis of feedback. They must. It is part of the systems as they have been conceptualized and as they operate in America today. The fact that educators or school-board members *may* pay attention to the feedback does not negate the fact that there is nothing in the system which *requires* them to do so at all. And anyone familiar with education knows hundreds of examples which suggest that evaluative data are often ignored completely.

How many times have school systems employed consultants to evaluate their building needs or mathematics programs or reading programs, and then refused to pay attention to the recommendations? Why has such a situation developed in American education? Why have we been unable to contrive an educational effort patterned after the other social systems which are so characteristic of "the American way?"

THE EDUCATIONAL DILEMMA

Several problem factors are inherent in the educational dilemma. Three will be considered here: (1) a false concept of professionalism, (2) a false concept of local control, and (3) an apparent conflict of purpose in thinking of science as a device for control. These problems are described below.

False Concept of Professionalism

All groups which are truly professional use the power of professionalism to achieve the purposes they pursue. In education, however, being professional is sometimes equated with being loyal (e.g., carrying out administrators' decrees); being dependable (e.g., reporting to work on time, preparing reports accurately and quickly, adhering to the curriculum guide); or studying for additional degrees. These factors are probably related to professionalism in some way, but under no circumstances do activities such as these embrace the real meaning of the term.

Professionalism involves at least four things: service to others, making judgments, an ethical code, and the use of organization to impose a discipline upon those who veer from the written code. In groups which are truly professional, practitioners adhere to the ethical way; i.e., perform the essential service for others in the most effective manner known. In this sense, the concept of professionalism embodies the elements of altruism to an appreciable degree. Those persons who are professional define the professional act and the professional group so that the persons being served can be assured of the highest possible quality of service. Professionalism is essential in the effectiveness sense; it enables those whose tasks involve helping others fulfill their role in the most effective way. This concept of professionalism seldom characterizes the teaching group.

False Concept of Local Control

Local control in education in the United States dates back to the early colonial days and is still considered to be operative in most places today. The notion is only partially true, though. One state superintendent has gone so far as to describe it as "the myth of local control." Any consideration of the available data suggests that the control of any local school lies at least as much beyond the local borders as it does within them.

In the first place, education is a function of the state government in every state. School districts are established by the state, schools accredited by the state, teachers certified by the state, school sites approved by the state, buildings inspected by the state, school expenditures audited by the state, and much of the financial support provided by state.

This is not to deny the fact that certain important controls operate at the local level, because they do. Important curriculum policies and decisions and methodological considerations are prime examples of local control.

But the national government exerts considerable control, too. Through its various incentive programs, the national government exerts influence over local schools in the areas of what is taught (e.g., vocational and technical education); what equipment is used (e.g., language laboratories, television sets, and microscopes obtained through NDEA funds); what techniques will be employed (e.g., NSF institutes train foreign language teachers to use the audio-lingual method rather than the traditional approach); and in other ways.

The point is, local educators and school boards have felt that local control would enable them to make evaluative decisions about what occurs in the schools. This has fostered the misconception that those who *plan* and those who *do* can also adequately perform the evaluative function. The New York State Board of Regents is an important exception, but the concept of local control that is most often accepted is indeed false.

Science, Democracy, and Control

The concerns for democracy and science in education have often been at cross purposes in the operation of schools. Seeking to break from the harsh and rigid authoritarian approaches often evidenced in schools of the past, educators attempted to move toward child-centered approaches and non-punitive techniques to help students learn. In the process of this shift, many persons became sensitive to such ideas as "force" or "control."

About the same time, however, new developments in behavioral science offered educators new knowledge and new tools with which to pursue their goals. Research in biology, psychology, anthropology, and sociology gave educators insights into the problems of growth and learning; many began to adopt the methods of science to study problems in the educational field.

As education became more scientific, however, the age-old conflict between the humanities and the sciences again arose. Science as a process seeks to describe and define in order to predict and thus control. Building inductively from empirical fact to generalization to scientific law, scientists are inevitably concerned with the problems of both prediction and control. Educators, however, shy from words like "predict" or "control." When the labels are applied to whole groups (e.g., predicting the success of the freshman class in college on the basis of scholastic aptitude scores) or socially undesirable types (e.g., controlling juvenile delinquents) they are acceptable, but the idea of predicting precisely what eighth-grader Sue Jones will do when confronted with a particular stimulus in a classroom seems to smack of authoritarian control and a denial of free will.

The fact is, even though they have been encouraged to do so, teachers are reluctant to specify their objectives precisely and in behavioral terms. If they did, then their evaluations of student achievement would imply that they either did or did not achieve their educational goal. If the children failed to learn (i.e., achieve the objective specified), this would also mean that the teacher failed. On the other hand, if the objectives were achieved, this would mean that children had learned but that they had also been controlled; that is, they were not free to miss the educational goal. Either alternative would be disturbing to a dedicated teacher. No teacher likes to think of himself as ineffective and unsuccessful in attaining his educational goal. In the same way, however, no teacher likes to think of himself as openly manipulating children and forcing them to achieve particular goals—that is obvious control and not "democratic," in most teachers' minds. This problem contributes to the educational dilemma: to be effective means to control, whereas to be ineffective means to do a poor job. Thus, vague statements of purposes and loose generalizations regarding educational objectives are made—and efforts to assess the effectiveness of the educational effort are almost always bound to fail.

SUMMARY

Education is a social system. Social systems which are most effective involve different groups in the planning and doing and evaluating roles. Those systems which are most productive and responsive utilize the feedback data in corrective ways. The educational system, however, has a basic flaw. There is no separate group which assumes the evaluating role. This problem is further compounded because many educators are prisoners of the terms they use:

"professional," "local control," "democracy," "science," and "control." Chapters Four and Five explore two sets of ideas designed to overcome some of these problems related to educational change.

Chapter Four

Untangling the Theoretical Dimensions

INTRODUCTION

The logic of the argument is clear. Educators recognize a need for change. They have attempted many kinds of change. These changes have been less than satisfactory from almost every point of view. As a social system, education seems unable to process pertinent data so that appropriate and effective changes can be assured.

In many ways, the educational operation in America seems inconsistent with those fundamental concepts of democracy and science and free enterprise which have made our nation great and strong. The purpose of this chapter is to explore these concepts with the hope of identifying the crucial dimensions which make them effective. Principles from this analysis will then be applied to the development of a theoretical rationale which might be applied to education. This chapter, then, represents an effort to conceptualize a "theoretical" model or rationale for educational change.

THE THEORETICAL DIMENSIONS

What is republican-type government? What is science? What is the free enterprise economic system? What are the essential ingredients or elements which characterize these human undertakings as the dynamic, powerful, social systems which they are?

In a logical analysis, our systems of government, science, and industry yield five different dimensions: goal, domain, function, confidence, and record. In some instances, these dimensions are obvious and, therefore, easily identifiable. In other cases, they are much more difficult to find and to describe. In the sections which follow, each of these five dimensions is considered with the idea of developing theoretical principles which might apply to the problem of promoting significant educational change.

The Goal Dimension

As stated in the Preamble of our Constitution, the purpose of our government is "to form a more perfect Union, establish Justice, insure domestic Tranquility, provide for the common defence, promote the general Welfare, and secure the Blessings of Liberty to ourselves and our Posterity." In this way, the Constitution sets forth general goals which give direction to our form of government. The remaining portions of the Constitution extend these general goals and, at the same time, spell out precisely the procedures whereby they are to be achieved. For the purpose of this discussion, however, the point is that there *are* specific objectives for our government, and that these objectives appear in written form, primarily in the Preamble and the Amendments to the Constitution. As such, they constitute tangible evidence of exactly which purposes are legitimate and should be pursued.

In the field of science, the basic goal is the attainment of "truth." Different scientists define "truth" in different ways, but for most it represents reality, or that which is. The basic purpose of science, therefore, is to comprehend and understand and map out reality—to come to grips with what exists.

The basic purpose of the economic enterprise as we know it in this country is to make money: to show profit. Unless the individual or organization engaged in economic activity can show financial gain, the basic objective has not been realized. If a company loses money, its goal is immediately recognized as having not been attained. On the other hand, if an organization does show a profit during a particular period of time, it is acknowledged as having achieved the goal.

This discussion has a very simple point: every social system has goals. These goals may be stated explicitly or they may be implicit and described only in general terms. But every social system reflects activities which are designed to achieve particular purposes, and if one traces out those activities, the goal dimension can always be found.

The Domain Dimension

The concept of federalism is an accepted and meaningful aspect of our governmental enterprise. In terms of "spheres of influence," certain activities are reserved to the national government, some to the state government, some to county governmental units, some to cities and towns, and some activities are reserved to individual citizens. This separation of realms of authority creates an interrelationship among the various levels of government which is essentially spatial in nature; it is a geographical concept, in the main. The national government coins money and regulates commerce, the state government assumes jurisdiction in criminal cases, and local governments assume responsibility for traffic control, building codes, and sewage disposal, for example. In other areas, the responsibility is joint in nature (e.g., highway construction, financing education, and airport management), but in every case, the delineation of authority is precise. Thus, the federal government may pay 86 per cent of the cost of a new interstate highway, and the state government may pay the remaining 14 per cent. State governments may have jurisdiction involving stolen property, until such property is transported across state lines—then the federal authorities become involved. Federalism represents the domain dimension of republican-type government as we know it in the United States today.

In science, the domain dimension is reflected in the various disciplines themselves. Geology is different from biology, which differs from sociology, which differs from physics, which differs from chemistry, and so on. The domain of each science involves that segment of reality which has been singled out for investigation and study by the scientists in that particular field. Though there is some overlap, the notion of disciplines or fields of inquiry represents the domain idea as it applies to the scientific field.

Each corporation in industry represents a different domain. General Electric and Westinghouse both produce electrical equipment, for example, but they are different companies. Each is unique. Ford Motor Company is different from Chrysler Corporation or American Motors. One department store is different from another department store. In each case, the areas occupied by the various companies differ. They are housed in different buildings. The products which they produce are different. The persons involved in the manufacturing or distribution process are not the same. Each corporation is a separate, unique entity.

These illustrations all suggest that one important dimension of these social systems might be thought of in terms of the domain they occupy or serve. Spatial separation according to area or sphere of authority appears to be one factor which characterizes the groups identified for study here.

The Function Dimension

If it is possible to think of the spatial differentiation between aspects of government, science, and industry, in the very same way one can also think of differentiation which applies to the functions which are performed. In government, for example, the notion of "separation of powers" implies a clear delineation of authority in terms of function. Legislatures make the laws, executives carry out the laws, and courts interpret the laws. These various functions are not the same.

Similarly, the methods of science are such that formulating hypotheses, testing hypotheses, and making inferences from data are all different, too. Platt describes the approach of science in the following terms:

> In its separate elements, strong inference is just the simple and old-fashioned method of inductive inference that goes back to Francis Bacon. The steps are familiar to every college student and are practiced, off and on, by every scientist. The difference comes in their systematic application. Strong inference consists of applying the following steps to every problem in science, formally and explicitly and regularly:
> 1. Devising alternative hypotheses;
> 2. Devising a crucial experiment (or several of them), with alternative possible outcomes, each of which will, as nearly as possible, exclude one or more of the hypotheses;
> 3. Carrying out the experiment so as to get a clean result;
> 1'. Recycling the procedure, making subhypotheses or sequential hypotheses to refine the possibilities that remain; and so on.[1]

In industry, the functional dimension is portrayed by the different kinds of industrial enterprises: mining, automobile production, electrical appliances, home construction, laundry, restaurants, and the like. In each instance, the variation in function is evident in terms of the kind of product or service which is produced.

The functional dimension represents an important aspect of the social systems we have described. In its own unique way, each social system embodies a differentiation of function or methodological approach. When the particular methods are applied to the particular domain, the objectives or goals are hopefully attained.

The Confidence Dimension

A fourth aspect of every social system involves the extent and manner in which that social system deals with the matter of public confidence. The confidence dimension, in fact, might be labeled "trust-distrust," in that each so-

---

[1] John R. Platt, "Strong Inference," *Science,* CXLVI (October 16, 1964), 347.

cial system seems to have a way of balancing these two elements precisely and effectively.

In government, for instance, that concept which we recognize as "checks and balances" represents the confidence dimension. All governmental operation is conceived in such a way that authority is shared among the various elements involved so that each branch of the government has a certain sphere of authority as reflected in the separation of powers dimension. But this sphere of authority can only be exercised in accordance with authority which is derived from other branches of the government. For example, the President appoints members of the Supreme Court, with the advice and consent of the Senate. This interrelationship of authority is one illustration of the way in which balance of power is maintained in our concept of federalism. Another illustration is reflected in the fact that the President is Commander in Chief of the armed forces, but appropriations which are necessary to maintain the armed forces are granted by the legislature, and never for periods to exceed two years.

In the area of science, the confidence dimension is reflected in several ways, but probably it is best illustrated in the concept of replication. That is, when a scientist publishes a research report, his peers are able to repeat the experiment to find out whether his observations are correct. In this way, science is able to progress and make gains in the pursuit of truth. By repeatedly subjecting phenomena to rigorous examination, scientists are able to ascertain exactly what is so. Here we see a beautiful illustration of the way in which scientists build on distrust, in much the same way as Jefferson used the notion of distrust in his conceptualizations of government.[2]

In the field of business and industry, the confidence dimension is reflected in the terms "goodwill," "brand names," and in the fact of competition. A basic concept of modern advertising is that people can be taught to depend upon the integrity of the producer. The fact that the consumer is always free to select another product forces the producer to operate in such a way that he must gain the

---

[2]Saulk K. Padover, *Thomas Jefferson on Democracy* (New York: Mentor Books, 1939), p. 93.

confidence of his buyers; he cannot simply demand it as would be the case in a monopolistic market.

The Record Dimension

Social systems can also be characterized by the kinds of records they maintain. In government, for instance, laws are a matter of record, and they are codified. Court decisions based upon these laws are also organized and handled in a permanent record form. Indeed, one of the basic tenets of our governmental concept is that we are a government of laws rather than one of men. This notion implies that laws exist apart from men rather than in the minds of men, and even though men write laws and interpret and enforce them, because laws exist in a tangible, permanent, recognizable form, our nation is a better one.

In the area of science, publication of results becomes the written record. When a scientist conducts a piece of research, makes certain observations, and generates certain data, science can move forward and make progress only if those data are recorded in some tangible form. Scientists do not depend upon word of mouth to disseminate information, even though conferences and reading papers are a very important part of every scientist's life. Once a research study has been effected, the researcher describes it as carefully and completely as he can. After the manuscript is published, other persons interested and knowledgeable in that same field may then replicate the research themselves. Replication is only possible if the study has been described in sufficient detail for another researcher in a distant laboratory to undertake the same experiment in a comparable way. The concept of "publish or perish" has a broader meaning than that commonly attributed to it. One can build a powerful argument that if a scientist does research and does generate new knowledge, but does not share all that he knows by publishing the results, he is creating a danger for the human race. By not making available in written form the best evidence that he has at hand, he can, in fact, impede the progress of science, and in our day and age, that may mean that the human race might perish. In other words, survival in today's world does depend upon the best that men know, and the scientist is obliged to publish his results. He must or *all men* lose.

In the business field, the written record is the balance sheet. If the company makes money, the balance sheet reflects this fact. If the company loses money, the balance sheet shows that, too. In either case, the balance sheet exists. It describes precisely both the extent and the direction of accomplishment in fiscal terms.

The record dimension reflects those aspects of the social system which provide the corrective feedback data by which the system can benefit and improve and grow. It is at this point, in other words, that the evaluation process manifests itself. And because it manifests itself in tangible form—that is, in written form—the data are real and observable. They can be manipulated, studied, talked about, and examined carefully and critically. By their very nature, records must deal precisely with the stated objectives reflected in the goal dimension described earlier. For the system to be complete, in other words, the goals must be described in such a way that someone can ultimately ascertain whether or not they have been achieved.

Summary

The purpose of the discussion thus far has been to suggest that every social system has five dimensions: a goal dimension, a domain dimension, a function dimension, a confidence dimension, and a record dimension. Table 1 describes these various dimensions as they apply to the examples of government, science, and industry. It immediately becomes evident that social systems which differ as much as these obviously do, are nonetheless very similar conceptually. This would seem to suggest that there may be principles inherent in each of these conceptualizations which can be lifted out and applied to the field of education.

RECONCEPTUALIZING THE EDUCATIONAL SYSTEM

From this analysis, it seems obvious that education as a social system is inadequately conceived. This does not mean that someone is to blame. On the contrary, the inadequacy is more the result of an incomplete evolution of the concept in our society than it is the fault of any one person or any one group. Even so, if the inadequacies do indeed exist, it now becomes the responsibility of thoughtful persons who are concerned about education in the broadest sense to devote their energies to the problem and attempt to devise an appropriate remedy. The remaining portion of this chapter will set forth what seem to be reasonable inferences based on the discussion thus far.

In general terms, education needs to be rebuilt in such a way that all of the previously described dimensions are embodied within the system. At present, it is evident that education not only does not include all of these dimensions, but, in fact, it does not include most of them. This situation must be changed. Furthermore, these dimensions must be built into the educational operation in such a way that they are dynamically related and functionally effective. The very concept of education as a social system requires that the interrelationship possess these qualities. In other words, if education as a social system is to be a responsive, sensitive, evolving enterprise, adapting to the needs and the pressures of the times, incorporating the best of its own experience, and eliminating what has proven unsuccessful or ineffective, then it is essential that the full power of the systems concept be built into education in such a way that the system possesses the power of self-renewal and self-generation and self-improvement. These are the central ingredients of effective social systems; without them, the power of the systems concept would be lost.

Can We Clarify Educational Goals?

Let us begin with a discussion of the goal dimension. Education is not without purpose. There are goals and there are objectives. The fact is, however, that as a nation, state, university, school district, or as an individual school, goals and purposes are seldom stated explicitly and with precision. Under the umbrella of pluralism, some persons even argue that goals ought not to be stated. In the opinion of this author, goals must be stated in explicit terms, and they should relate specifically to students' learn-

TABLE 1

Conceptual Dimensions of Various Social Systems

Social System	Goal Dimension	Domain Dimension	Function Dimension	Confidence Dimension	Record Dimension
Government	Constitution	Federalism	Separation of Power	Checks and Balances	Laws and Court Decisions
Science	Truth	Disciplines	Hypothesizing Experimenting Inferring	Replication	Publication of Results
Industry	Profit	Corporations	Various kinds of Industries and Services	Competition and "Goodwill"	Balance Sheet

ing. To assume that implicit educational purposes will be either widely understood, attained, or evaluated in terms of learning is naive.

One would think that "helping children learn" would be as acceptable and widely understood as "making a profit" is in business. This is not true, however. Many of the decisions which occur in education do not relate to student learning at all. Rather, they pertain to "teacher welfare" or "administrative authority" or "school-board prerogative" or "decreased costs of operation" or some other concern. It cannot be assumed that the basic purpose of education is to help students learn, nor can it be assumed further that this objective is paramount and central in the eyes of all. The basic purposes of education must be spelled out in writing for all to see.

What we need is a kind of "educational constitution" which sets forth a statement of educational purposes. Ideally, this educational constitution should be voted upon by the population at large. That is, for the public school system of any state, for instance, there probably should exist in written form a statement of the educational objectives of that state which should be submitted to the voters of that state in a referendum and approved by the body politic. Before such an activity could occur, of course, it would be necessary to have a kind of "educational-constitution convention," but ultimately the results or platform of that conference should be submitted to the voters of that state for their support and their approval.

General assemblies of one kind or another are often held to discuss educational purposes, but because a "White House Conference on Education" or a "State House Conference on Education" does not submit the results of its deliberations to the general public for its approval, or because such groups are not empowered to act for the people of that region, all that typically results is fine talk and worthwhile experiences for the particular people who were invited. Most educators would concur, however, that such conferences and such deliberations seldom have any significant effect upon the educational endeavor "out there." The idea of a conference to clarify purposes is sound. What is needed now is a deliberate effort to incorporate the purposes into a written statement which would be recognized by the public and have their support.

Furthermore, if these goals were stated in general terms, much like the purposes of government are stated in the Constitution, and if they deliberately incorporated the pluralistic notion as an avowed purpose, then the possibility of diversity, creativity, and ingenuity would be assured. However, if the goals were also stated in learning terms; that is, for example, to "help students learn," then when it became necessary to make judgments about the effectiveness of the operation, such factors as teacher satisfaction, economic efficiency, or extent of participation in a particular program would become inconsequential. If the crucial goal of educational systems is "helping children learn," and if this goal could be spelled out in sufficient detail to give both substance and direction to the educational enterprise, then the possibility of the system functioning effectively might be realized.

On the other hand, when the goals are implicit rather than explicit, then it becomes feasible for school systems, institutions of higher education, or classroom teachers to make interpretations in terms of what they *think* the important educational objectives are. In this way, the concerns of economics, teacher satisfaction, or administrative preference all have the possibility of being given more attention and greater significance than they should. The educational system must have a clear statement of educational purposes and it must appear in written form. Further, these purposes must bear the stamp of approval of the people who are behind the system. This constitutes one significant way in which the system presently needs to be changed.

What Are the Educational Domains?

If we look now at the domain dimension, it seems fairly evident that this is one place in which the educational system is already fairly adequate. Spatially, we have separated those aspects of education which are different and have made them discrete. School districts typically do not overlap. One university is different from another university. Elementary education is different from secondary education, and the like. Within universities, there are spatial differences between colleges, between departments, and between areas within departments. For the time being, at least, we shall grant that the domain dimension has been satisfactorily achieved.

Can We Clarify the Functional Domain?

In terms of the functional dimension, it is immediately evident that extensive overlap exists. Chapter Three was devoted to a discussion of the inadequacies of the functional dimension as they presently exist in education. We have very little separation of power according to function. What is needed is a clear statement of who makes policy, who carries out that policy, and who judges the effectiveness of that policy. Furthermore, if the concept is to be complete, it is also important that each function is accomplished by a different group and that each group has power.

What Is the Confidence Dimension in Education?

What kind of elements would be appropriate in the reconceptualization of the educational system in terms of the confidence dimension? Can we accept the notion of distrust as not only desirable but as an extremely important element in education? This would not mean, of course, that educators should "breed" distrust. Hardly. It does mean, however, that skepticism is important, and that, as a social system, education must have built into it an opportunity for the skeptic to be heard.

The concept of science involves *dis*proving hypotheses. The concept of free expression which our society provides guarantees that the skeptic's point of view can always be heard. We want to guarantee unto ourselves the benefit of criticism so that we may progress. The concept of free choice in economics is predicated upon the fact that the individual consumer can choose *not* to buy a particular product or accept a particular service. It is this negative aspect which gives power to the system. In education, therefore, we must incorporate the notion of criticism into the operation in such a way that the criticism can be put to the test. If it is valid, the criticism must be dealt with; the wrong pointed out must be righted. If it is not valid, then the system must be so conceived that it does not have to pay attention to negative feedback which does not apply. It should be possible to borrow principles from law, economics, and science in order to apply them to education on this point. For the moment, perhaps it will suffice that this dimension is visible—that we know, understand, and appreciate the importance of the idea in it. If we can accept the notion of distrust as an essential ingredient for the improvement of all education, then we are well on our way toward constructing a new theory which will capitalize upon the essence of this idea.

Can We Build a Record Dimension?

Finally, our reconceived system must include a written record. We could not have a government of laws rather than a government of men without the codification of laws and the organization of court decisions. In the same way, the operational aspect of education must include a systematic and comprehensive procedure for collecting data regarding the effectiveness of the system. Furthermore, these data must be so organized and so made available and so utilized that they are brought to bear precisely upon the educational tasks which are involved. That is, given that one of the basic tenets of the educational constitution described above is to help children learn, and given that helping children learn is described in specific terms, then it becomes necessary to collect information relative to whether or not this learning has occurred. Furthermore, this information must be real. It must be tangible. It must be public property. It must relate specifically to the ends described.

In addition, education as a social system must be built so that this information is used. Such data dare not be ignored. Availability is important, but it certainly is not enough. The record dimension must contain those elements of understandability, particularity, and permanency which characterize scientific publications, balance sheets, or court decisions in our judicial process in America. It cannot be comprised of vague impressions, guesses, or loose interpretations. It cannot reside in the mind of one man or a few persons. It cannot be implicit in any respect. For the concept of social systems to be maximally effective, the record dimension must be both tangible and specific, and it must be utilized in such a way that the tangibility and the specificity are the elements which give substance to the corrective feedback.

Summary

Education as a social system must be reconceived. The goals and purposes must be stated with precision and must be adopted by those who are concerned. There must be both a spatial and a functional separation of power and these power sources must be so related that the element of distrust is built into their operation in such a way that the system can improve. Finally, there must be a written record of the entire proceedings.

These five elements, only one of which presently seems to be incorporated into education to any appreciable degree, must be made part and parcel of the educational system of tomorrow.

The remaining chapter of this book is devoted to a discussion of several proposals for educational change. One of these proposals relates to public education. One relates to higher education. One relates to teacher education. One relates to the profession at large. And one relates to curriculum changes within a school district. As these proposals are read, they should be viewed as *possible* kinds of change—new kinds of *hypotheses for change*—not finished, polished constructs. In no way are these ideas to be construed as definitive proposals for change. They are suggestions.

Because the concept of education as a fully functioning social system has only recently come into full view, efforts to translate the concepts into reality are undoubtedly incomplete and imperfect, but hopefully a step in the right direction. In some instances, the ideas represent a sub-system of a larger system. Just as the concept of quality control has been built into and adopted by industry in order to insure maximum effectiveness of the operation, so too does the concept of professionalism represent an internal effort to improve. It is a kind of sub-system to the larger system, and it utilizes the same principles as

Untangling the Theoretical Dimensions

the systems concept itself employs. As a sub-system, however, it never really comes to the acid test. For example, the quality-control engineers in a particular industry might have every assurance that their product is the best, but unless the public buys the product, it makes little difference what the quality-control engineer says. The real test in business or industry is whether or not the general public buys the product or service which is provided. Even so, the concept of quality control is obviously an important idea, and it has enabled American industry to keep closer tabs on itself in order to make the acid test more viable and more productive.

In the very same way, the medical industry as a social system employs the concept of professionalism to keep the members of the profession focused on the effectiveness goal. When the pathologists' reports are discussed in meetings of the hospital surgical staff, the activities of particular surgeons or physicians are scrutinized from an internal point of view. Likewise, if a patient complains of being overcharged or calls attention to some violation of ethical practice to the county medical society, the grievance committee of the medical organization attempts to bring the full power of professional ethics to bear upon the practitioners involved. Examples of peer approval of projects in science could also be made. The point is, as a social system, education must be carefully reconceived. As a part of this reconceptualization, if we can build into the new concept sub-systems which incorporate the same principles of systems operation which have been described *thus far,* we ought to be able to generate a notion of education which has infinitely more power than the concept which presently prevails. The purpose of the chapter which follows is to describe in practical terms the implications of the concepts which have been developed up to this point.

Chapter Five

Propositions for Educational Change

INTRODUCTION

In general terms, our change efforts in education have been inadequate because education as a social system has been incomplete. Some of the dimensions of more complete systems have been identified in the last chapter, and the purpose of this chapter will be to consider possibilities for bringing integrity to the educational system in various ways.

Several propositions for educational change will be described. These ideas represent outlines of promising hypotheses to improve the process and structure for educational change. But hypotheses and propositions should be tested, not accepted as dogma or rejected out of hand.

Because each learner is unique in terms of his purposes, motivations, and creative experiences, the task of providing adequate, effective instruction for millions of students is an unbelievably complicated chore. When this is added to the fact that there are thousands of "systems" in half a hundred states, all involving an approach to education which is compulsory rather than optional, the problems become even more intricate. If education were a minor operation with only a few people involved, and if it were optional and not required, then the task of bringing about appropriate change would be easier and more effective.

But the reality is otherwise. Thus, it seems inappropriate to suggest any one solution or one kind of educational change. A redundancy of change efforts, in fact, is probably to be desired.

INTEGRITY OF THE EDUCATIONAL SYSTEM

In the Bible, the prophet Isaiah declares that "the Lord is our judge, the Lord is our lawgiver, the Lord is our king; he will save us" (Isaiah 33:22). Freud's conception of the id, ego, and the superego as the planning, accomplishing, and evaluating aspects of personality represents the same three functions as they pertain to one man rather than to the universe. It may be reasonable to presume that one man can satisfactorily accomplish these diverse functions as they relate to himself alone. It may be reasonable, too, to presume that God's infinite wisdom, infinite capacity, and infinite skill enable Him to cope with the entire universe in the very same way.

But educators are not God. Furthermore, the institutions with which they deal are much more elaborate and much more complex than an individual human being, if only because thousands and thousands of individual human beings are involved. Those social systems which have integrity and which are more fully functioning in a democratic way than education have devised ways of separating and sharing authority according to function rather than consolidating power in a few persons' hands. Outlined graphically, a social system with integrity—that is, one which is whole and concerned with truth—might look something like that pictured in Figure 1. A social system which is complete, viable, and self correcting (i.e., concerned with truth) is valid. It has integrity.

But the educational system is incomplete. It is not necessarily self-correcting. It is not conceptually whole. It lacks integrity, in other words.

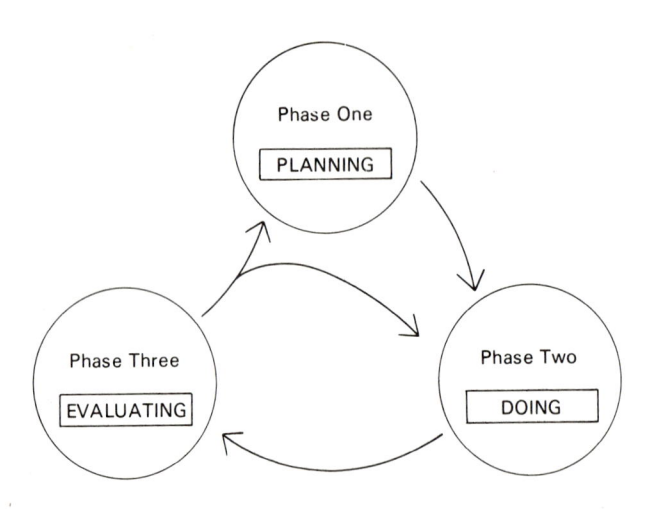

```
        Phase One
        PLANNING


Phase Three          Phase Two
EVALUATING           DOING
```

Figure 1

Diagram of a Social System with Integrity

It has been said that "war is too important to be left to the military men." In a similar way, education is too important to be left to the educators. But it is also too important to be left to the experts, or politicians, or businessmen, or any single group. Education is a social system with which all men must be concerned. We must rethink the purposes, structure, and functions of education. We must find ways to build integrity into the system. Men with integrity in education are not enough. We must conceptualize and operationalize a system of education which is both complete and concerned with truth. We must build integrity into the *system*, in other words. Figure 2 describes the educational system as it exists and functions presently. We should conceptualize either a series of processes or a series of groups to fill the phase-three void. Or, better yet, we should do both.

If we actually established a group and gave them authority of their own, we would complete the system conceptually. If those persons who now serve in educational roles devised or utilized evaluative procedures and data to change and improve education within the framework of the system as it now exists, that would be a step

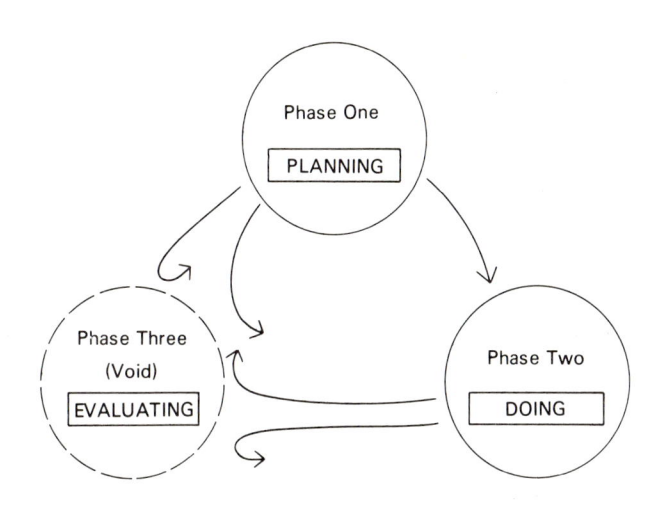

Figure 2

Education as a Functioning Social System

in the direction of making the system function in a more effective way, even though conceptually it would still be incomplete. And if we took a series of steps along both of these routes, we would most assuredly have an educational system which would be dynamic, responsive, and changing to improve.

REDUNDANCY OF EVALUATIVE FUNCTION

What is being suggested, of course, is a kind of redundancy of evaluative function within education. Consider how evaluation occurs in other social systems to help those systems improve.

The medical field for example, has a series of evaluative functions which are accomplished in various ways to keep the system alive and changing. First of all, the practice of medicine and the allied fields (e.g., pharmaceuticals, medical insurance, and the like) operate within the framework of our free enterprise system of economics. There is nothing compulsory about medical treatment, or which physician a person may choose, or which drug a physician must prescribe. Evaluation of the service or product is accomplished by using dollars as ballots and voting for or against a particular service or product. If a physician is ineffective, his practice will be negatively affected. If the drug is not helpful, it will tend not to be prescribed. Ineffective physicians go out of business or change their ways. Drug or insurance companies which do not meet the needs of those they serve must change or they, too, will be forced out of business. The field of medicine benefits, in other words, by virtue of the fact that the economic framework within which it functions generates feedback data which enable those within the system to improve through change.

But there are additional evaluation approaches within the medical field which also accomplish the same purpose. For instance, physicians have also developed an elaborate series of checks on themselves in their professional activities. Being "truly professional" involves a great many factors, not the least of which is supervision and control of the members by the professional group.[1] There are at least five ways in which this peer control manifests itself among medical men: rigid requirements for admission to medical school, certification by the state according to examinations prepared by practicing physicians, grievance committees within the county medical society to receive and process complaints, tissues committees within the hospital in which surgeons supervise their fellow surgeons on the basis of empirical and clinical data provided in the pathologists' reports, and utilization committees within hospitals which check on the way physicians use the resources and staff of the hospital to provide high-quality medical care.

The intent here is simply to outline the elaborateness and the detail which are part of the "truly professional" posture and activities of physicians. Obviously, some physicians behave in unethical ways. Obviously, some grievance committees shield shoddy practice and charlatanism. But the existence and function of such committees is typically effective and generally real. Furthermore, the supervision of physicians by physicians does not presume a "legal line of authority" as is true in education. That is, competence is not measured by a someone higher

---

[1] Jack R. Frymier, "Professionalism in Context," *Ohio State Law Journal*, XXVI (1965), 53-65.

up on the "line of authority" ladder. The hospital administrator never tells the surgeon how to operate or the radiologist how to interpret X rays. Professional authority in medicine is rooted in competence rather than the legal power of the state to require persons to comply.

The medical field has other evaluation groups, too. The Pure Food and Drug Administration, for example, is another regulatory-type group which independently assesses the quality and safety of particular foods or drugs. And the PFDA has power: it can direct that certain foods or drugs not be used or only used under given conditions.

In the social system we call "government," we have the obvious advantage of judicial review as a means of keeping our governmental system dynamic and open to change. Recent court decisions relative to civil rights and prisoner's rights, for instance, have resulted in extensive changes in police procedures, interrogation, educational opportunities, employment opportunities, and the like. Some persons quarrel with the power which the courts in our country exercise, but few would deny that courts generate feedback data which are new and which are utilized. And though it does not work perfectly, most persons in this country feel "free" (i.e., they are not afraid to move about the country freely or speak freely or change jobs or enter strange and unfamiliar places) because they have confidence in our "government of law" and its associated judicial procedures. Part of this confidence stems from our tradition (i.e., our experience with the system), but most of it comes from the formality and ritual of the judicial process itself. If a person were to be arrested tomorrow for a crime he did not commit, he would typically have confidence in "the system" to set him free. That confidence would arise from his knowledge of the fact that he is entitled to a fair trial, to counsel, to cross-examine witnesses, to present evidence, and to appeal. The formal aspects of the system, in other words, give confidence to those who are involved that "truth will out" and "justice will prevail."

Administrative review is another device within the system of government which causes our system to be responsive to feedback data and to improve.[2] When an individual

---

[2] Walter Gellhorn, *When Americans Complain* (Cambridge: Harvard University Press, 1966).

feels that he has been slighted or wronged, he can "go over the head" of the person responsible and try to get the situation or conditions changed. Suggestion boxes and complaint departments are examples of administrative review in practice.

The "Ombudsman" idea is still another variation which has been added to the governmental systems in some foreign countries and in a few local governments within the United States.[3] In most cases, the Ombudsman is one man appointed by the legislature with a charge to consider complaints or initiate review in any aspect of the social sphere in which he feels people have been wronged. He typically functions as a kind of investigative court and serves the role of collecting, interpreting, and providing feedback to the rest of the system so that it can improve itself through change.

Legislative review in the form of congressional or senate hearings represents another way in which our system of government uses evaluative feedback (e.g., the censures of Senators McCarthy and Dodd in recent years).

The same idea appears in business and industry in various forms. The free enterprise concept is obvious, but Better Business Bureaus, quality control engineers, and the Sherman Anti-Trust Act all represent instances in which evaluations and assessments are made and the feedback data are utilized to help the whole system improve.

The basic point of this entire discussion is that no one approach or single group or one technique for generating and using assessment-type data is adequate. Redundancy in terms of the evaluative function is necessary and desired. The more procedures there are for collecting and interpreting information about how the operation is going and where it is going and why, the better the system will be. That is, those systems which have elaborate and extensive feedback mechanisms and which are conceptualized in such a way that the feedback data must be utilized have the greatest integrity as functional systems. They are complete. They are concerned with truth. They are viable operations in every way.

One way to describe redundancy within a social system is by reference to sub-systems as portrayed graphically

---

[3] Walter Gellhorn, *Ombudsman and Others in Nine Countries* (Cambridge: Harvard University Press, 1967).

Propositions for Educational Change 69

in Figure 3. Such a concept can be extended almost indefinitely. The point which is most important here is twofold: First, redundancy as multiplicity in terms of assessment function defines, sharpens, and polishes the operation of the total system so that it simply must get better. It must improve. Second, redundancy as a series of sub-systems within a larger system means that the system itself is open rather than closed because the sub-systems have "feelers" which extend out into the other systems of the world.

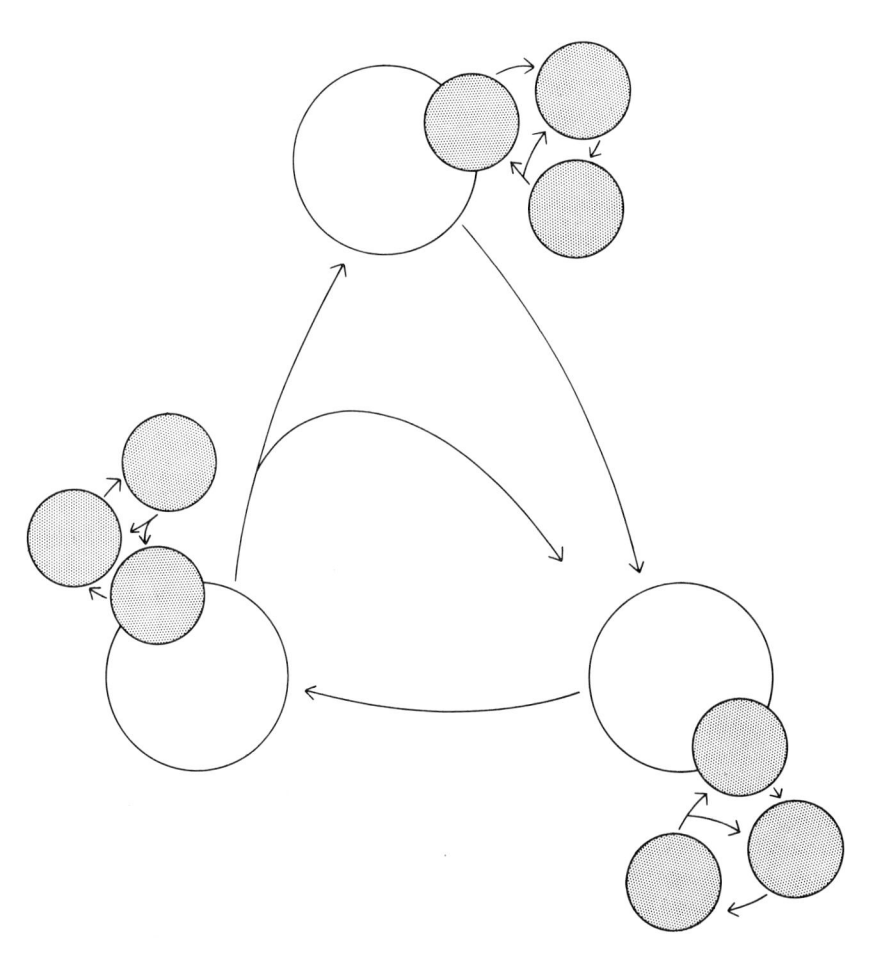

Figure 3

Sub-Systems Within a System

When one confronts the systems concept initially, it seems to be "closed." The fact of the matter is, any system which is broadly conceived tends to be "closed." The kind of "system" with which we are here concerned, however, must be viewed as part of a larger system. That fact, plus the theoretical possibility that evaluative redundancy keeps the system both more open and more responsive, should give us important insights about how to modify the educational system so that it absolutely must improve.

SOME PROPOSITIONS REGARDING CHANGE

It was said before, but it must be said again: Even though the propositions which follow describe specific details and very precise procedures, they are illustrative, not definitive. They are suggestions and ideas that might be thought about and tried. They are not *the* answer. They may not even be *an* answer. They are interesting and hopefully significant ideas which grow out of the general concept which has been set forth in this book.

Changing Public Education

The state legislature should enact legislation establishing within each school district within the state an education assessment council. In this same legislation, the legislature should also establish a state education assessment council. Each council should include seven members, about half of whom should be professional educators with the other half comprised of lay persons. One person should be designated as executive officer for the group, and it probably should be stipulated that this person's training should be in the area of educational research or evaluation. Each local district's education assessment council should be appointed by the superintendent with the approval of the governing board, but should not be directly responsible to either the superintendent or the board. To assure their autonomy, each educational assessment council should receive two per cent of the current operating budget as adopted by the governing board of the district involved. Members of the assessment councils should serve for six-year terms, and these terms of office should be staggered so they do not generally coincide with one another or with the terms of the school-board members.

The legislation should stipulate that the basic purpose of the local district's education assessment council should be to assess the effectiveness of education within that district. Furthermore, this council should be given the power to pass judgment on the appropriateness and validity of the educational policies which are adopted by the governing board or on the way in which policies are implemented by the professional staff.

At the state level, the state superintendent of education should appoint, with the approval of the state board of education, a state education assessment council. Some reasonable sum of money should be made available regularly to this group. As before, this group should not be directly responsible either to the state superintendent or to the state governing board; the authority of all three should be equal.

The basic purpose of the state education assessment council should be two-fold: First, it should have the responsibility and authority to assess educational policy or the way in which policy is implemented at the state level. Second, it should function in an appellate role by reconsidering certain decisions reached by the assessment councils of local districts. In other words, if a particular school district's education assessment council considers a particular policy and finds that policy to be educationally unsound, it should have the authority to declare that policy null and void and to direct the superintendent and his professional staff to vacate that policy or rule it from the books and from practice in the schools. However, should the school district's governing board so desire, they should have the opportunity to appeal that decision to a higher "educational court." The state education assessment council should serve that appellate role.

Figure 4 describes this concept in graphic terms. Here we see a picture of education within a state as a complete social system which is a part of a larger social system (i.e., the state itself). In the outer circle we see the fundamental branches of the state government: legislative, executive, and judicial. Education is a state concept, therefore it must be viewed within this larger social sys-

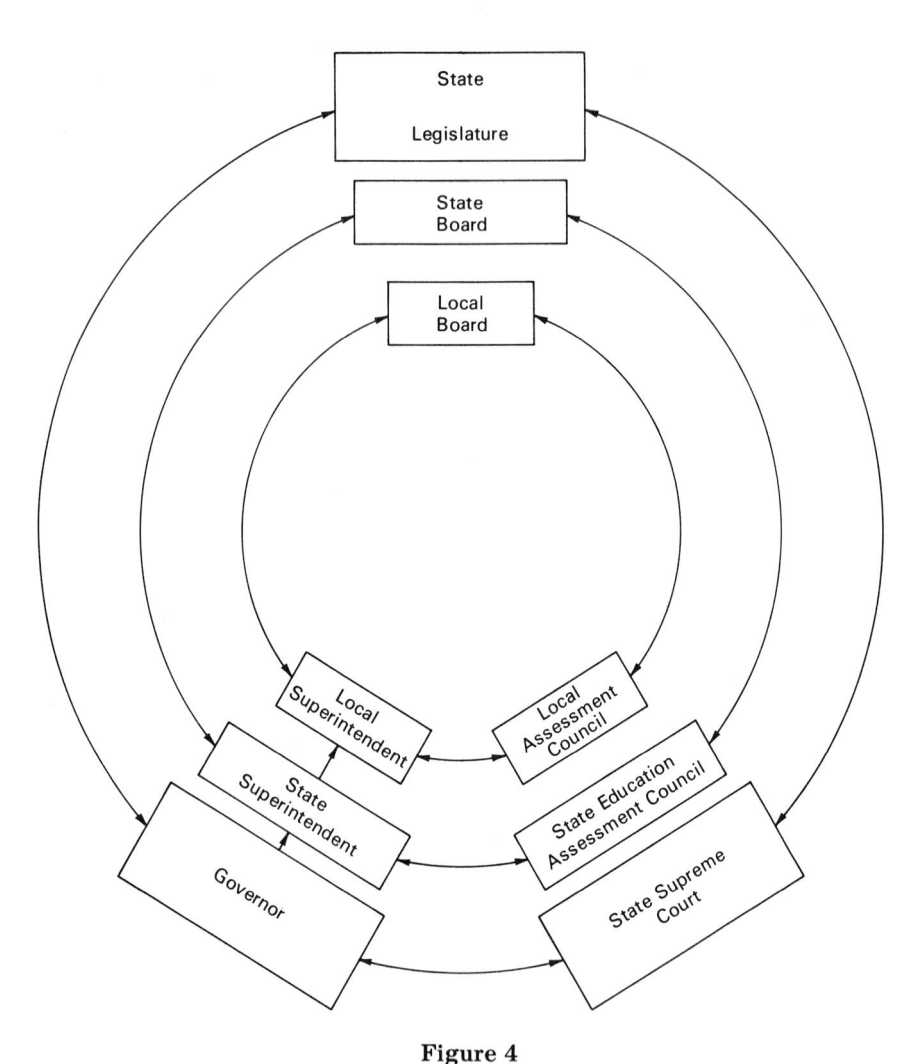

Figure 4

Education as a Fully Functioning System

tems construct. Within the second circle are the state educational governing board, the state superintendent, and the state education assessment council. The governing board would perform the policy-making or planning role. The state superintendent and his staff would perform the implementing or doing role. The state assessment council would accomplish the evaluation and infering role.

At the local level, the same functional concept would prevail. And though it is not shown here, still another set of groups within the district circle could easily be imagined. In other words, within each building there could be a planning group (e.g., many schools now have a faculty steering committee or parent advisory council), the principal would represent the chief officer of the implementing group, and an assessment group could be established within each school building. It does not seem appropriate that such an idea should be legislated from the state level, but the establishment of the concept by the local district would certainly be in keeping with the theory.

This graphic concept of education as a fully functioning social system illustrates several of the ideas which have been previously outlined. For example, there is separation of power according to function. This is the most obvious point. There is also separation of power according to geography—the domain dimension. The picture also shows the interrelatedness and the interdependence reflected in the concept of checks and balances—the confidence dimension. The goal dimension and the record dimension are not shown. As in government, industry, or science, these dimensions must be developed over time as the result of certain ways of working.

Changing Higher Education

The university should establish a university assessment council within the framework of its constitution or bylaws. Each college within the university should also establish a college assessment council, and departments within the colleges should be encouraged to establish standing assessment committees where practicable. The university and college councils should include five members appointed jointly by the faculty councils and chief administrators of the various units involved. The basic purpose of the assessment councils should be to assess the effectiveness of the university and its colleges in attaining their purposes.

The specific functions and responsibilities of each of these groups should be specified in the university constitution and college bylaws. Terms of office, renumeration, and specific duties would be difficult to delineate here, but it is most certain that assessment councils should not be directly responsible either to the administrators or to the policy-making groups. Adequate provision for the independent functioning of such assessment councils would have to be assured. In other words, it should not be possible for arbitrary administrators or boards of trustees or individual professors to exert undue influence upon such councils through withholding of financial support, failure to promote, etc. This idea is portrayed graphically in Figure 5.

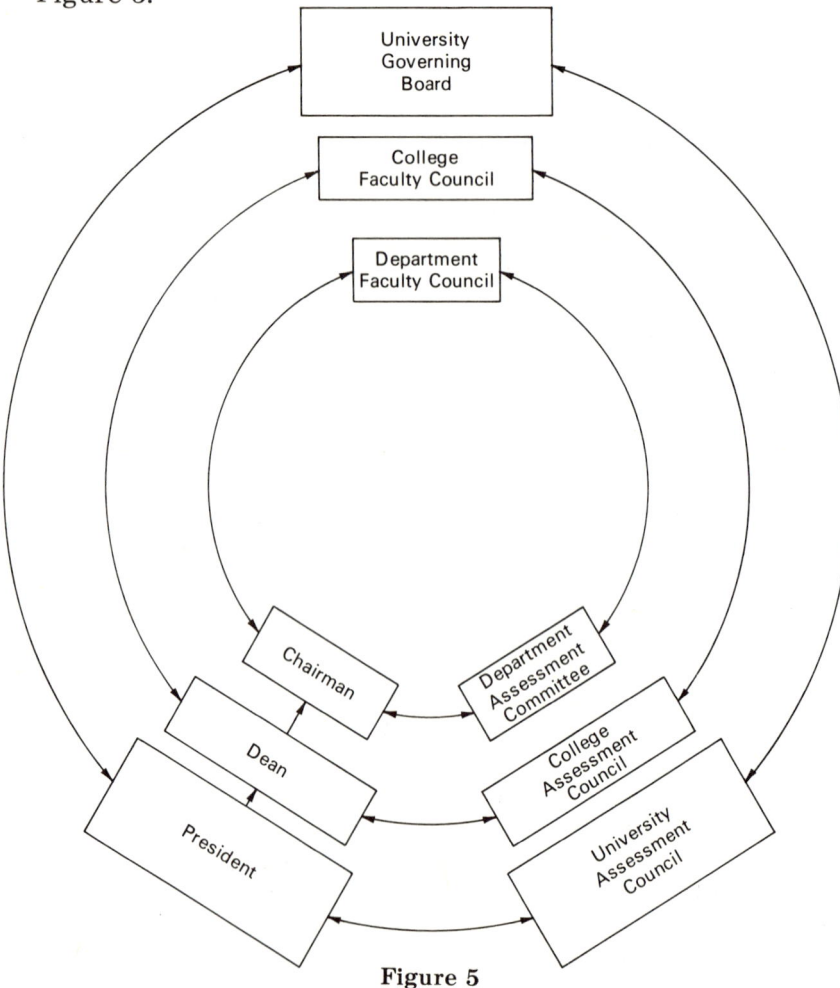

Figure 5
The University as a Fully Functioning Social System

Propositions for Educational Change 75

One illustration of how part of such a conceptual scheme might look when mapped out in more detail is available as Appendix B. In that section, a set of bylaws for one college within a university is described, including a college assessment council along with a statement of its organization and functions. Therefore, no further attempt will be made here to suggest specific factors about organization or function. The fact is, each institution of higher learning is unique. It has its own mission and its own tradition, and these forces act as forward pull and backward drag at the very same time. Institutions interested in incorporating such evaluation and assessment procedures into their ongoing operation could conceptualize organizational structures which would fit their particular history and needs. The Weber Report may be very helpful to institutions interested in considering such developments.[4] For example, the eighth recommendation of this report states:

> A formal appeals procedure should be established to resolve disputes involving individual faculty members and the administration.
> The substantitive scope of the appeals procedure should be determined by the academic senate.
> The appeals procedure may make provision for neutral third-party intervention, including arbitration.[5]

In the proposal suggested in this book, the "third party" would be an established part of the university system, and it would assess problem areas in addition to those involving disputes. However, both the Weber Report and this book build upon the "third-party" idea, as well as the notion of building improvements out of negative concerns. Without going into specific detail, it will suffice to say that progress and improvement in higher education can grow out of problem areas, conflict, and concern, if the institution has a formalized way of receiving and processing criticism-type data. Assessment councils may comprise one such way.

---

[4]Arnold R. Weber, et al., *Faculty Participation in Academic Governance,* (Washington, D. C.: American Association for Higher Education, 1967).
[5]*Ibid.,* p. 3.

Moving Toward Truly Professional Status

The two propositions outlined to this point—changing public education and changing higher education—both involve modifications of the educational systems which are involved. Changing the basic systems will be difficult. Such factors as tradition, vested interest, and caution will inevitably exert influence. There are some changes within the system, however, that might be effected with a lesser degree of difficulty. Moving toward truly professional status would involve several such changes. The propositions sketched out below are not detailed, but it is hoped that the "flavor" of the idea might be gained and that such propositions might generate further thought and creative effort in the directions which are implied. Three sets of ideas are described: selection and training (pre-service education); organizational activities (inservice education, including self-discipline and peer control); and curriculum research (a programmatic-type of quality control).

Selecting and preparing prospective teachers is a very important and very difficult responsibility. Two things are inherent in the proposition here: selection and training must include a consideration of what motivates people to enter the teaching profession and stay; and the pre-service education must be drastically overhauled.

Although the figures are not easily accessible, it is probably safe to say that fewer than half of those who enter college teacher-education programs complete those programs, and fewer than half of those who graduate enter teaching and stay. The attrition rate is fantastic. To reduce this attrition, colleges of education should move to establish six-year teacher education programs: four years of undergraduate education and two years of professional schooling. The number of persons admitted to professional schools should be sharply curtailed. Theoretically, such changes should result in fewer persons entering teacher-education programs (therefore providing more opportunity for universities to concentrate their resources in order to do a better job of preparing persons to enter the field). However, such changes should also result in more persons entering the profession and staying for longer periods of time (their greater commitment would result in their increased proficiency and ability to command better salaries). Requiring a four-year degree and a rigid selection procedure before admittance to a program of professional preparation should eliminate from teacher education all of those "sweet young things" and "culls" and "misfits" who want a college degree but are not really interested in entering teaching with a commitment to stay or to develop expertise and competence based upon extensive training and experience in the field. Screening procedures should include personality assessment as well as determination of intellectual ability and academic achievement, since rigid, inflexible persons will be psychologically incapable of adaptation and change over the years.

Those who are admitted to professional schools of education should be prepared to be generalists first and specialists later. After they have developed conceptual and technical competence in working with individual students of all age levels and in all subject-matter areas, then they should specialize in a subject area and do further work with students at an age level in which they are most interested and concerned.

If a prospective teacher experienced a professional preparation program which required him to become a "general practitioner of teaching" and competent to work with youngsters of various ages and in a variety of content areas, understanding of the developmental aspects of learning and the "whole" of education should enable him to make rational and serious commitments relative to whom and what he would really like to teach. Two full years of study *after* the general education program also would mean that professional schools of education would not have to "bootleg" professional courses into a regular four-year program at the expense of the liberal arts program. It would also mean that the professional program could concern itself with "professional" preparation, unburdened by the "academic respectability" which is often characterized by "term papers" and "Mickey Mouse" work serving no meaningful purpose. Professional preparation could teach the methods, techniques, and skills so essential to any truly professional person's daily role. That which distinguishes a surgeon from a physiologist, for example, is not the degree to which each knows the subject matter. They are both very competent regarding the structure and function of the human organism. But the surgeon has an additional set of skills: the methods and techniques which are peculiar to surgery. The physiologist does not have these skills. An extended program of preparation would enable teacher educators to develop particular competencies and skills in prospective teachers to a much greater degree.

The second facet of the proposal to achieve truly professional status involves organizational efforts to extend pre-service training through a program of continuous upgrading (inservice education), and through an active program which would include admission to and expulsion from the profession through self-discipline by the professional organization and peer control.[6] Greenwood makes the point precisely when he says:

> Every profession has a built-in regulative code which compels ethical behavior on the part of its members.... Through its ethical code the professions' commitment to the social welfare becomes a matter of public record, thereby insuring for itself the continued confidence of the community.[7]

At another point Greenwood maintains:

> The ethics governing colleague relationships demand behavior that is cooperative, equalitarian, and supportive. Members of a profession share technical knowledge with each other. Any advance in theory and practice made by one professional is quickly disseminated to colleagues through the professional associations.[8]

In this sense, all of the usual things which professional organizations generally tend to do at the national level (e.g., report recent research findings, generate dialogue regarding innovations and correct practice, use "experts"

---

[6]Jack R. Frymier, *The Nature of Educational Method* (Columbus, Ohio: Charles E. Merrill Books, 1965), Chap. 10. See also Myron Lieberman, *Education as a Profession* (Englewood Cliffs, N.J.: Prentice-Hall, Inc., 1956) and T. M. Stinnett and Albert J. Huggett, *Professional Problems of Teachers* (New York: The Macmillan Company, 1963).

[7]Ernest Greenwood, "Attributes of a Profession," *Social Work*, II (July, 1957), 44-55 as reprinted in H. M. Vollmer and D. L. Mills, eds., *Professionalization* (Englewood Cliffs, N.J.: Prentice-Hall, Inc., 1966), p. 14.

[8]*Ibid.*, p. 15.

and "consultants" to synthesize research results, etc.) could also be accomplished at both the local and state level by the professional organization itself. The local professional organization, in other words, should assume primary responsibility for inservice education and supervision of its members. Supervisors should be employed by and responsible to the professional organization to help teachers improve. Work-days, conferences, use of consultants, and other types of inservice efforts should be undertaken by and be the responsibility of the professional organization rather than the school district as such.[9] Obviously, the financial aspects would be considerable, but such efforts are essential if educators are ever to achieve truly professional status. If the responsibility remains where it presently is, teachers and others will continue to assume that "those who are higher up know more than those who are lower down" on the scale. The members of the teaching profession must understand that authority in a profession should be based on competence rather than on law and that they must find ways to improve themselves. In the final analysis, this means that they must assume responsibility for supervising themselves in both a regulatory and a growth-oriented way.

The task of the professional organization is two-fold: they must devise means for coping with unethical activities, and they must devise means for coping with ineffective activities. Figure 6 outlines in general terms what such procedures might look like operationally. A detailed discussion will not be attempted at this point, but it should be mentioned that formal procedures might be conceptualized within the framework of the professional organization which would then cope with problems of ethics or effectiveness. Further, there could be opportunity for review by other professional groups, and necessary action could be instituted by the appropriate *professional* (rather than legal) agency.

If such an organizational effort were initiated, and if the activities were conducted apart from public view (i.e., discreetly by members of the professional committees in-

---

[9]Sam Leles, "Evolving a Theory of Effectiveness in Education" (Ph.D. dissertation, The Ohio State University, 1967), p. 162.

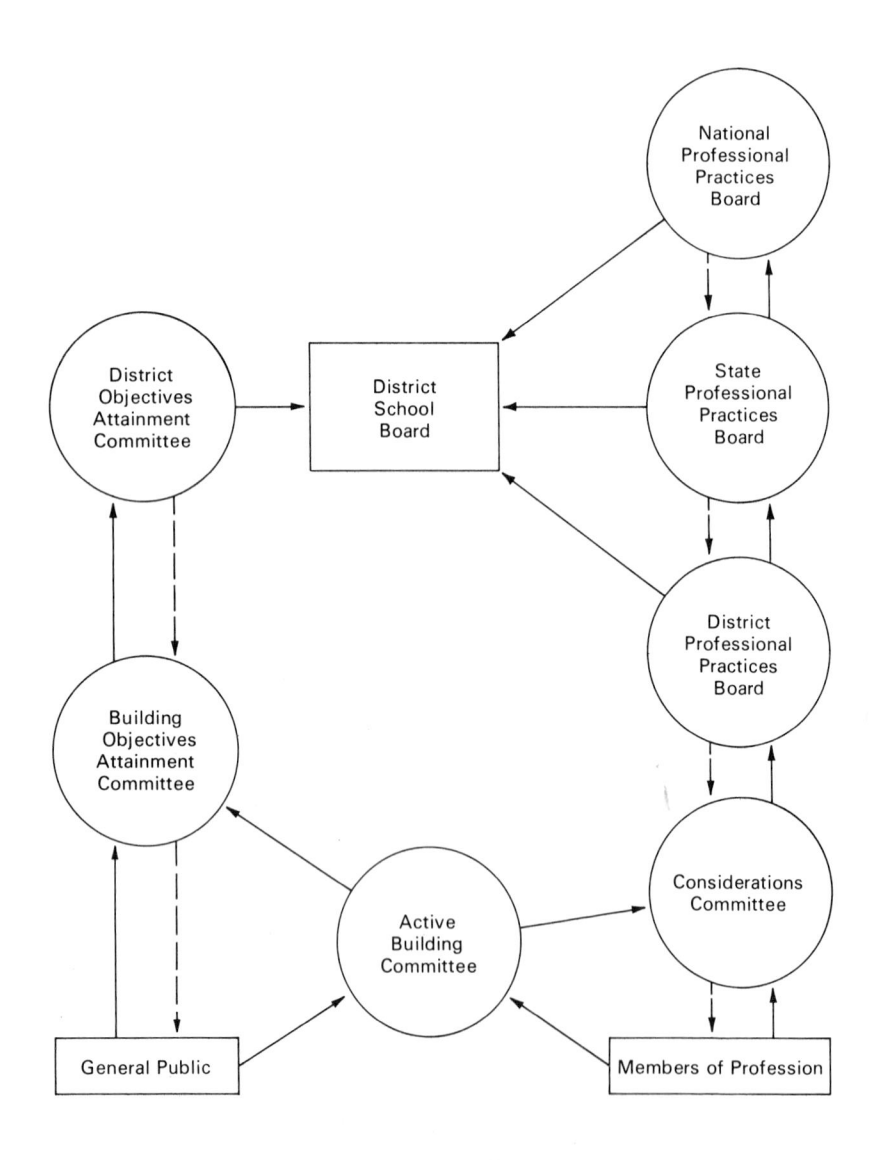

Figure 6

Professional Organizational Structure to Improve Education

volved), effective pressure could be brought to bear upon professionals whose conduct or activities were adjudged ineffective or unethical or both. Furthermore, such efforts could be accomplished by the professional organization act-ing completely upon its own. The essence of truly professional behavior includes members assuming responsibility for policing their own ranks for the benefit and protection of the persons served—in this case students. Appendix C spells out in more detail just how such a concept might be operationalized.

The third facet of the proposal to achieve truly professional status involves the development of a system of program evaluation and curriculum research. Appendix D outlines how a professional organization might propose policy to the governing board which would commit the local district to a plan of curriculum improvement based upon clearly stated assumptions, democratic-type involvement, and research-type procedures. Such a plan would enable districts to obtain continuous and valid feedback data regarding the ongoing operation. Thus, decisions of a policy nature or an implementing nature could be based on empirical fact rather than tradition or "expert" judgment or the legal authority of those involved.

SOME FINAL OBSERVATIONS REGARDING CHANGE

Education is a social system. Any social system is concerned with both ends and means. Feedback is the relationship between ends and means. Feedback is the process by which an organism or an organization assesses what it is doing and what it ought to be doing. Those organisms and those organizations which are capable of adaptation, growth, and change have highly refined sensing mechanisms for ascertaining what they ought to be doing (ends) and how well they are accomplishing those goals (means). In other words, feedback is the mechanism by which they measure the gap between their performance and some standard of performance; those systems which are fully functioning use these feedback data as bases for action to close the gap between the objective and the actual performance.[10]

Educational endeavors must evaluate what they do in terms of their objectives. Measuring input factors (e.g., books in the library, proportion of staff with advanced de-

---

[10] Van Rensselaer Potter, "Society and Science," *Science*, CXLVI (November 20, 1964), 1018-1022.

grees, teacher-student ratio) as indices of objectives attained is not the way.[11] "Freezing" input factors through legislation, accreditation, or negotiation processes (e.g., maximum class size, number of books in library per student, number of minutes per course per week for so many weeks per year) may have some relevance to the effectiveness of the educational system involved, but there is little except tradition or pooled opinion to suggest that such conditions make much difference in the lives and minds of those who are taught, even though they may satisfy the teachers or others who are concerned.

The educational system must be changed. In effecting a new system, there must be a deliberate and rational distribution of authority according to function, rather than consolidation of authority according to tradition or whim. Furthermore, the newly conceptualized system must be built to withstand maximum stress and strain. Just as bridges, airplanes, or governments are built to withstand and handle maximum rather than average or typical strain, the educational system must also be responsive, adaptive, and capable of coping with all kinds of pressures and forces.

In the past, we have confused the strength and integrity of the system with the strength and integrity of the people who work within it. Actually, both are extremely important, but we dare not presume that "good" men are enough to make the educational effort effective. Hoping that "good" men can bring about significant and positive educational change when the system itself is inadequate and incapable of change is to guarantee frustration and failure for all concerned. Knowledge grows like organisms, with data serving as food to be assimilated rather than merely stored.[12] Education as a social system must utilize feedback data for purposes of improvement.

Criticism and feedback data are essential to progress. Both democracy and science convert criticism to positive advantage. Our "government of laws"[13] and the "integrity

---

[11]John A. Perkins, "Which College is Best?" *Saturday Review*, (September 11, 1965), pp. 71-82.

[12]Paul Weiss, "Knowledge: A Growth Process," *Science*, CXXXI (June 10, 1960), 1716-1719.

[13]Edward S. Corwin, ed., "Introduction," *Constitution of the United States* (Washington, D. C.: U. S. Government Printing Office), 1953, p. xviii.

of science"[14] both involve the institutionalization of rational means to achieve given objectives. But the institutionalizations require that feedback data which are generated be used to help the systems work more effectively and improve.

This book has outlined the forces, need, and the efforts to improve education through change. It was determined that the educational system is inadequate. It lacks integrity. It is incomplete. There is no formalized process or group which uses feedback data systematically and effectively to enable the educational system to improve. Several propositions for educational change have been described. These ideas could be tried. Both the analyses and syntheses presented here have concerned themselves with the integrity of education: its viability, its completeness, its concern for truth. Those who are responsible for its operation must lead the way toward building integrity into the educational system.

The most noble purpose of education is to prepare the rulers of the state. In the United States, that means the education of us all, for we are rulers of our state. The educational system must be improved if we are to cope with the complex problems of today and tomorrow. This book has outlined one kind of rationale for educational change.

---

[14]Barry Commoner, *et al.*, "The Integrity of Science," *American Scientist*, LIII (June, 1965).

Appendix A

Annotated Bibliography

On the pages which follow are a number of research studies which illustrate the kind of evidence referred to in Chapter Two regarding "hypotheses for change." These studies have been arranged alphabetically according to author, and each includes a brief abstract of the research procedures and results. This listing is not meant to be a comprehensive review of the literature; rather, it should be considered as illustrative of the type and range of research reports which are available in the area of curriculum change.

Bibliography

1. Aftreth, Orville B. and Donald G. MacEachern. "An Action Research Study in Arithmetic," *The Arithmetic Teacher,* XI (January, 1964), 30-32.

    The specific problem identified by the staff and members of the PTA Educational Enrichment Committee was to compare the effects of an accelerated program of instruction with an enriched program of instruction on achievement in arithmetic at the fourth-grade level. Both fourth-grade classes at Sidney Pratt School, San Diego, California, and their teachers were selected for participation in the study. The two programs of instruction resulted in substantially the same performance on standardized tests in arithmetic reasoning and computation. The two methods appeared to be equally effective with high and average achievers. The accelerated method was probably inappropriate for use with low achievers.

2. Alder, Henry L. and Donald A. Norton. "Intermediate Algebra in High School or in College? A Statistical Analysis," *Journal of Educational Research,* LII (October, 1958).

    Three classes taught by different instructors, in a course in elementary probability and statistics with a total of 150 students, made up the subjects. There was a strong indication that students who did not take a second year of high school algebra were not necessarily those with inferior mathematical talent, yet it seemed that they faced a serious disadvantage in their college mathematics courses which could not be overcome by a one-semester college course in intermediate algebra.

3. Allen, Edward D. "The Effect of the Language Laboratory on the Development of Skills in a Foreign Language," *Modern Language Journal,* XLIV (December, 1960), 355-357.

Fifty-four tenth-and eleventh-grade pupils were studied. The non-lab group received the material the lab group was using, but the non-lab group read it and answered questions in writing. Those students who spent 20 per cent of their time listening and speaking French or Spanish in the laboratory achieved significantly higher scores in reading, vocabulary, and grammar.

4. Alter, Millicant. "Retention as a Function of Length of Retention Interval, Intelligence, and Training Time," *Journal of Programmed Instruction,* II (Summer, 1963), 7-17.

    The subjects were 236 students ranging in grade from seven to eleven, taking mathematics courses in six different schools. The data did not reveal that fast learners exhibit better retention than slow learners. Initial proficiency emerges as the prime determinant of delayed proficiency.

5. Altmiller, W. R. *et al.* "A Status Study of the Schools of the Western States Small Schools Project." A joint doctoral dissertation at the Colorado State College, 1963, 686 pp.

    Nineteen schools were evaluated in person by the team members. Median class sizes were Secondary-18, and Elementary-22. Most schools had very poor libraries and curricular emphasis was college preparatory. STEP and SCAT scores of students were at or above national averages—high in math and science, low in reading and verbal ability.

6. Amidon, Edmund and Ned Flanders. "The Effects of Direct and Indirect Teacher Influence on Dependent-prone Students Learning Geometry," *Journal of Educational Psychology,* LII, No. 4 (1961), 286-291.

    This study involved dependent-prone, eighth-grade students who were exposed to consistently direct vs. indirect styles of teaching while learning geometry. The dependent-prone students learned more in the classroom in which the teacher gave fewer directions, less criticisms, less lecturing, more praise, and asked more questions which increased their verbal behavior. Compared with students in general, dependent-prone students were apparently more sensitive to the influence pattern of a geometry teacher.

Appendix A

7. Amidon, Edmund and Michael Giammateo. "The Verbal Behavior of Superior Teachers," *Elementary School Journal*, LXV, No. 5 (February, 1965), 283-285.

   All 153 teachers were observed by a trained observer who used the Flander's System of Interaction Analysis. The observer categorized the verbal behavior of teachers and pupils during the language-arts period. The verbal patterns of superior teachers could be identified and these patterns did not differ markedly from the verbal behavior patterns of other teachers.

8. Anderson, George R. and Abram W. VanderMeer. "A Comparative Study of the Effectiveness of Lessons on the Slide Rule Presented via Television and in Person," *The Mathematics Teacher*, XLVII (1954), 323-326.

   Five classes of high school sophomores were involved in the experiment. While the mean score on the final test made by the group taught "in person" was approximately 3.5 percentage points higher than that of the group taught by television, this difference was not statistically significant. It would seem that teaching the slide rule via television was practically as effective as teaching it in person. Television classes did not have the advantage of interclass discussion under the direction of the instructor.

9. Anderson, Kenneth E., Fred S. Montgomery, and Sid F. Moore. "An Evaluation of the Introductory Chemistry Course on Film," *Science Education*, XLV (April, 1961), 254-269.

   Thirty-three chemistry classes in five high schools in Wichita, Kansas participated. There were 590 students who completed all phases of the study. The students in the non-film classes achieved more than did the students in the film classes. Four out of the nine comparisons were significant and in favor of the non-film groups. Only two of the nine comparisons were signigicant and in favor of the film groups.

10. Anderson, Robert H. "The Influence of an In-Service Improvement Program upon Teacher Test Behavior and Classroom Procedure," *Journal of Educational Research*, XLIV (November, 1950), 205-215.

Thirty-three teachers made up the sample group. Thirty teachers made up the control group. While the results were not statistically significant, it was concluded that in-service improvement of teachers was a long-term process and that, in the beginning, in-service programs should focus on practical problems, deferring theoretical considerations until later.

11. Arthur, Grade. "A Study of the Achievement of Sixty Grade 1 Repeaters as Compared with that of Non-Repeaters of the Same Mental Age," *Journal of Experimental Education*, V (December, 1936), 203-205.

    This study was an attempt to determine what a child, who has not yet formed a habit of failure, accomplishes when forced to repeat a grade. Sixty Grade 1 repeaters of a small public school system were the subjects. The average repeater of the group studied learned no more in two years than did the average non-repeater of the same mental age in one year.

12. Baden, Walter D. "The Focus on the High School, 1957-62: An Analysis of Changes in Curriculum Balance in Four Selected Senior High Schools on Long Island, New York, Since October 1957," *Dissertation Abstracts*, XXIV (February, 1964), 3159-3160.

    While science, mathematics, and foreign languages led in rate of change, English and social studies followed closely behind. Aside from the addition or deletion of courses, there was no curriculum change reported in any of the non-academic elective fields. The clearly greater focus on the five academic fields resulted in a shift in curriculum balance in that direction. Items directly related to pupils and the social pressures to which they were subject appeared to be a more significant reason for change than any other.

13. Barrilleaux, Louis E. "An Experiment on the Effects of Multiple Library Sources as Compared to the Use of a Basic Textbook in Junior High School Science," *Journal of Experimental Education,* XXXV (Spring, 1967), 27-35.

    Forty-two students as eighth-graders and later as ninth-graders were matched at the Malcolm Price Laboratory School, State College of Iowa. For all evaluations, effectiveness in terms of obtained means systemati-

Appendix A

cally favored library materials without a basic textbook. The comparative effect did not depend on the ability levels. The experimental group scored significantly higher in number of library visits, time devoted to library activities, participation in free reading, use of more library materials in science and non-science classes.

14. Bateman, Donald and Frank Zidonis. "The Effect of a Study of Transformational Grammar on the Writing of Ninth- and Tenth-Graders," *NCTE Research Report No. 6*. Champaign: National Council of Teachers of English, 1966.

    Fifty students who comprised the ninth-grade class (and, in the following year, the tenth grade) at the University School of The Ohio State University were used for the sample. Structural complexity scores of well-formed sentences and of malformed sentences revealed no significant differences between the groups. A knowledge of generative grammar enabled students to increase significantly the proportion of well-formed sentences they wrote.

15. Baxter, Joseph and Reginald Jones. "Superior High School Student Performance in a Program of Acceleration," *National Association of Secondary School Principals Bulletin*, XLVII (March, 1963), 13-25.

    How did high school students admitted to early college work fare academically as compared with regular college students? Superior students received no special treatment, but obtained grades in direct competition with regular college students, except for those enrolled off-campus. Superior student appraisal of themselves indicated that they had profited from participation. There was no significant difference, however.

16. Beasley, Kenneth L. "An Investigation of the Effect of Team Teaching Upon Achievement and Attitudes in United States History Classes," *Dissertation Abstracts*, XXIII (March, 1963), 3256.

    This study investigated team teaching in United States history at Evanston Township High School. There was no significant difference in the amount of subject-matter knowledge gained by students in team-teaching classes as compared to students in conventional classes. There was no significant difference of high and low levels of aptitude in team-teaching classes as compared to students of corresponding aptitude levels in conventional classes. The attitudes of students and teachers toward team teaching were essentially the same—positive.

17. Beinharn, D. E. "Balance of Education," *Educational Research Bulletin*, XL (October, 1961), 168-78.

This study took place in England at Oxford University with children in secondary grammar schools under both private and public control. They were in grades equivalent to the ninth and tenth in the United States. Two hundred fifteen students were tested in six different kinds of schools. A program separating children according to ability in England has produced educationally desirable advantages for bright children and disadvantages for the less able.

18. Belcastro, Frank P. "Programmed Learning: Relative Effectiveness of Four Techniques of Programming the Addition and Subtraction Axioms of Algebra," *Dissertation Abstracts*, XXIII, No. 3 (1962), 917-918.

Five treatment groups were equated as to intelligence, age, achievement in arithmetic reasoning, and achievement in reading using eighth-grade pupils. No technique was better than the Verbal Deductive Technique in teaching the addition and subtraction axioms of algebra for each level of intelligence, reading, and arithmetic achievement.

19. Bell, Terrell Howard. "Teaching Machines and Programmed Learning in Weber County," *Journal of Secondary Education*, XXXVII, No. 2 (February, 1962), 108-111.

Mathematics teaching loads were increased so that a mathematics teacher taught approximately 300 students per day and was relieved of clerical duties. Programmed learning appeared to have considerable promise in freeing teachers to serve in a more professional role with students.

20. Bennett, Lloyd M. "Comparison of Current Science Teaching Practices in Texas Junior High Schools," *School Science and Mathematics*, LXVI, No. 2 (February, 1966), 141-146.

Seven hundred and seventy junior high schools in Texas were contacted and 34 per cent responded. Significant differences in practices did exist in terms of the size of the school. Size produced greater differences in the procedures used than did the grade plan employed. Science classes were being grouped homogeneously on the basis of ability, but teacher recommendation as to group placement was becoming a more frequently used technique.

21. Benschoter, Reba P. and Don C. Charles. "Rentention of Classroom and Television Learning," *Journal of Applied Psychology*, XLI (1957), 253-256.

The original study on which this follow-up was based used 302 subjects: 54 took courses by TV at home and 248 were enrolled in campus classes. A total of 83 subjects were retested. There was no significant difference in amount remembered by the groups. Long-term retention of academic material learned by TV instruction was as good as that learned by traditional means of instruction.

22. Benson, Ronald L. and Don H. Blocher. "Evaluation of Developmental Counseling with Groups of Low Achievers in a High School Setting," *School Counselor*, XIV, No. 4 (March, 1967), 215-220.

Tenth-grade teachers identified at the counselor's request 28 boys who were low achievers and who had negative attitudes. Changes in academic grades were statistically significant in favor of the counseled group. Changes in disciplinary referrals favored the counseled group but were not statistically significant. Changes in feelings of adequacy were not statistically tested.

23. Berger, Irwin. "Improving Composition through Emphasis on Semantics and Critical Thinking," *Dissertation Abstracts*, XXVI (December, 1965), 3295-3296.

A group of 218 seniors participated in this study. Significant differences were shown between the honors-experiment groups and the honors-control groups, but not between the regular groups. Intelligence and aptitude were factors in learning the semantics-critical thinking materials.

24. Bicak, L. J. "Achievement in Eighth-Grade Science by Heterogeneous and Homogeneous Classes," *Science Education*, XLVIII (February, 1964), 13-22.

> In this study, three eighth-grade science classes at the University of Minnesota High School were selected to determine the effects of grouping by IQ level on science achievement. There were no significant differences in either overall science achievement or in an application of scientific knowledge between children in heterogeneous and homogeneous classes. There was no significant difference in the achievement of high members in low groups or low members in high groups. Low-ability students expressed discontent with their placement and wanted more demonstrations and experiments.

25. Bickel, Robert F. "A Study of the Effect of Television Instruction on the Science Achievement and Attitudes of Children in Grades Four, Five, and Six," *Dissertation Abstracts*, XXV (March-April, 1965), 5777.

> From three Cortland, New York elementary schools, 213 children were taught science via television and 219 children were in the control group. An analysis of mean science attitude scores revealed no statistically significant differences between the two groups.

26. Biersdorf, Kathryn Rooney. "The Effectiveness of Two Group Vocational Guidance Treatments," *Dissertation Abstracts*, XIX (1958), 163-164.

> The subjects were 71 male students recruited from introductory psychology and speech classes at the University of Maryland. Subjects in extended treatment showed significantly greater reduction in number of vocational problems in comparison with the control group. No other significant differences were found, although, four out of five criteria were in the predicted direction.

27. Bingham, N. Eldred. "A Study Made in Hillsborough County, Florida, to Determine What Science to Teach in the Junior High School." *Science Education*, XLVII, No. 3 (April, 1963), 226-236.

> The purpose of this study was to determine significant content of the science curriculum. A study group of

21 science teachers was used. Previous pupil experience influenced the selection of topics for inclusion in the curriculum. Students showed the least familiarity with the subject content of the earth sciences.

28. Blake, Robert W. "A Study of the Effectiveness of a Linguistics Approach in Teaching Punctuation to Secondary School English Students in Self-Instructional Units," *Dissertation Abstracts*, XXVII (1966), 2876-2877.

Sixty-five tenth-grade students from public schools were randomly assigned the linguistic units and another sixty-five were assigned the traditional units. There was no significant difference in achievement between the two groups. There was no difference in knowledge of punctuation between secondary school students who had self-instructional units in punctuation using a linguistics approach and students who had units using traditional materials.

29. Blankenship, Jacob Watson. "An Analysis of Certain Characteristics of Biology Teachers in Relation to Their Reactions to the BSCS Biology Program," *Dissertation Abstracts*, XXV (1964), 2877.

Seventy-five science teachers were the subjects of this study. There were no significant differences between science teachers who reacted favorably to the BSCS Biology Program and science teachers who reacted unfavorably. Teachers who ranked higher on measure of capacity for independent thought and action and who had taught high school biology for three years or less reacted favorably to the BSCS Program, while those who ranked lower on measures of capacity for independent thought and action reacted unfavorably to the program.

30. Blesh, T. Erwin and Alfred Scholz. "Ten-Year Survey of Physical Fitness Tests at Yale University," *Research Quarterly*, XXVIII (1957), 321-326.

This was a survey of the achievement of freshmen at Yale University on six tests of physical fitness which were administered as a part of the regular program of physical education. The data covered a period of ten years, 1947 to 1956, during which time approximately 10,000 undergraduates were tested. A skill requiring agility and body control, such as the fence vault, seemed to be quickly learned in comparison to the amount of time it took an individual to increase the strength of various muscle groups. It was shown that an individual's strength, agility, and coordination could be improved in a rather short period of time (12 weeks) where concentrated effort was placed upon that particular factor, and the exercises were at regular intervals.

31. Blinkenstaff, Channing B. and Frank J. Woerdehuff. "A Comparison of the Mono-Structural and Dialogue Approaches to the Teaching of College Spanish," *Modern Language Journal*, LI (January, 1967), 14-23.

The dialogue group achieved significantly more than the other group in reading and writing skills. There was no significant difference in either audio-lingual skills or in interest loss.

32. Bloomenshine, L. L. (A) "San Diego Uses the Teaching Team Approach in Staff Utilization," *NASSP Bulletin*, XLIII, No. 243 (January, 1959), 217-19. (B) "Team Teaching in San Diego," *NASSP Bulletin*, XLIV, No. 252 (January, 1960), 181-196.

The evaluation of the project was a subjective appraisal based primarily on reactions of the participants, observation of team-teaching activities, and sampling of the activities by means of a one-week time-diary prepared by the team members. No objective measuring instruments were used to determine the extent to which the quality of instruction was improved. Working as a team stimulated teachers to do a more effective job of teaching.

33. Bloomenshine, L. L. and Malcomb T. Brown. "San Diego, California, Conducts Two Year Experiment with Team Teaching," *National Association of Secondary School Principals*, XLV (January, 1961), 160-168.

Four schools participated in the project the first year; an additional school was added the second. Between 1,693 and 2,200 students participated. Achievement level was as high as for other regular classes of comparable ability in team teaching. Pupils had more opportunities to develop the ability to do independent research and teachers had more opportunities to meet the differential needs of high-ability and low-ability

Appendix A

pupils. Professional growth of the participating teachers was one of the most important outcomes of the project.

34. Boeck, Clarence H. "The Relative Efficiency of Reading and Demonstration Methods of Instruction in Developing Scientific Understanding," *Science Education*, XL, No. 2 (March, 1958), 92-97.

This study investigated the efficiency of three methods of science teaching: reading and discussion; demonstration only; and a combination of these methods. Reading and demonstrtion techniques were equally effective in producing learning as measured within the framework of this study. The demonstration method was given preference by the pupils, but was not more effective in producing learning as indicated by the measures provided.

35. Bowman, Herman J. "Perceived Leader Behavior Patterns and Their Relationships to Self-Perceived Variables—Responsibility, Authority, and Delegation," *Dissertation Abstracts,* XXV (1964), 3340.

Data from 100 subjects were included in the analyses. There were no significant differences in responsibility, authority, and delegation among respondents when elementary and secondary school principals, and when principals directly and indirectly responsible to chief school officers were analyzed. Selected groups of teachers in the school were better able to describe the behaviors of their principals than were the principals.

36. Boyd, Claude Collins. "A Study of the Relative Effectiveness of Selected Methods of In-Service Education for Elementary Teachers." Unpublished doctoral dissertation, University of Texas, 1961.

Ninety-six teachers of arithmetic in grades four, five, and six were used in the study. There was no significant difference among any of the (essentially) four groups of teachers under study. The methods used for training were televised instruction, lecture-discussion, and consultant services.

37. Brandon, James Rodger. "The Relative Effectiveness of the Lecture, Interview and Discussion Methods of Presenting Factual Information by Television," *Speech Monographs*, XXIII (1956), 118.

The methods of lecture, interview, and discussion were investigated to provide information for this study. There were 72 male and 72 female college students. The interview and discussion methods were significantly more interesting to the students than the lecture method when taken over the whole experiment. There was no significant difference in the amount of information communicated by each of the three methods. There was no significant difference in the amount of interest expressed in material presented in the first, middle, and last ten minutes of a half-hour television program.

38. Brown, B. Frank. *The Appropriate Placement School: A Sophisticated Nongraded Curriculum.* West Nyack, New York: Parker Publishing Co., Inc., 1965.

At the educational conference in May, 1963 at the Massachusetts Institute of Technology, the following conclusion was reached: an orderly curriculum scheme was needed to replace graded organization. The Appropriate Placement School championed a move from a curriculum for the group to a curriculum for the individual. Extreme changes in the manner in which teachers were assigned to work with students were called for. It was felt that reading was basic for learning in all subjects and that students must learn to read with precision and comprehension.

39. Bucher, Charles and Dominik Taddonio. "The Relationship Between the Physical Fitness Ratings of Aviation Cadets and Certain Early Life Experiences Pertaining to Physical Activity," *Research Quarterly,* XXX (1959), 136-143.

The Army Air Force Physical Fitness Test and a questionnaire were administered to 1,226 aviation cadets during World War II. Findings revealed a lack of appreciable differences in physical fitness in later years among the following cadets: (1) those who attended public, private, and parochial schools; (2) those who did and did not experience required physical education programs; (3) those who did and did not attend college; (4) those who lived in various geographical areas of the United States; and (5) those who lived in rural as opposed to urban environments. Some substantial differences were noticed relative to elementary school activities and to varsity sports participation.

Appendix A

40. Bundy, E. Wayne. "Television and the Learning of Spanish Verbs," in W. Schramm, ed., *The Impact of Educational Television*. Urbana: University of Illinois Press, 1960.

> The purpose of the study was to determine the effectiveness of instructional television presentational techniques as compared to conventional classroom procedures in promoting initial comprehension of critical basic Spanish verb-form concepts. Of 24 statistical comparisons made, 23 indicated a consistent trend favoring TV presentational techniques over conventional procedures.

41. Burkey, Betty and William Asher. "A Comparison of Ninth-Grade Accelerated Students and a Group of Tenth-Grade Students in Their Ability to Comprehend Biology," *Journal of Research in Science Teaching*, III (1965), 66-71.

> The data were derived from a study of 214 academic tenth-grade students and 30 ninth-grade students. Ninth-grade accelerated students who were moderately gifted performed as well, and better in some cases, than the matched group of tenth-grade students with whom they were compared under the same conditions and treatment. The teacher's judgment revealed that interest was higher and performance was better among ninth-grade pupils.

42. Burnet, MacCurdy. "Structural Grammar in English 101," *College English*, XV (April, 1954), 412-413.

> Sixty-five freshmen at Maryland State Teachers' College, Salisbury, made up the subjects for the first experiment; seventy freshmen made up the second. Conventional grammar was pedagogically faulty. Structural grammar was usable in the ordinary college classroom.

43. Cantrell, Sue Rowe and Loren T. Caldwell. "A Selection and Evaluation of Physics and Chemistry Concepts to be Used in the Seventh-and Eighth-Grade Science Program," *Science Education*, XLVII, No. 3 (April, 1963), 264-270.

> This was a study designed to develop an upgraded general science program for the junior high school. A representative concept from each area was evaluated in terms of frequency of occurrence in texts and its familiarity to seventh- and eighth-grade youngsters in terms of the facts and principles necessary for its

understanding. Seventh- and eighth-grade youngsters could handle representative concepts normally as part of ninth-grade science.

44. Carbone, Robert F. "A Comparison of Graded and Non-Graded Elementary Schools," *Elementary School Journal*, LXII (November, 1961), 82-86.

A sample of 122 non-graded pupils and 122 graded pupils was used. Pupils in the study were achieving above the national norms. In all areas of achievement and in total achievement, graded pupils scored significantly higher. Teachers in the non-graded schools appeared to operate much the same as teachers in the graded schools.

45. Carpenter, Paul W. and H. T. Fillmer. "A Comparison of Teaching Machines and Programmed Texts in the Teaching of Algebra I" *Journal of Educational Research*, LVIII (June, 1965), 218-221.

Subjects selected for participation in this investigation were 18 boys and 12 girls who had previously been enrolled in the enriched and accelerated seventh- and eighth-grade mathematics courses. There was no significant difference between the mathematical performance of a group of ninth-grade pupils studying Algebra I using teaching machines and a like group studying the same Algebra I program using programmed textbooks. There was no significant difference in time required to complete this course between the two groups of subjects.

46. Cassel, Russel N. and Max Jerman. "A Preliminary Evaluation of SMSG Instruction in Arithmetic and Algebra for 7th-, 8th-, and 9th-Grade Pupils," *California Journal of Educational Research*, XIV (November, 1963), 202-207.

This study was concerned with making a preliminary evaluation of SMSG developed instruction for four classes of seventh-grade arithmetic with 121 pupils, two classes of eighth-grade arithmetic with 63 pupils, and three classes of eighth- and ninth-grade Algebra I with 78 pupils by comparing test scores of such individuals with corresponding scores of pupils enrolled in traditional arithmetic and algebra classes. Pupils in SMSG instruction had statistically significant higher arithmetic and algebra test scores than those enrolled in traditional programs.

47. Castens, Anne Cole. "A Comparison of Two Organizational Approaches to Reading Instruction for Below-Grade-Level Readers in the Seventh Grade," *Dissertation Abstracts*, XXIV, 2733.

Fifty-seven seventh-grade pupils were identified as potential subjects by use of the Modern School Achievement Test. No statistically significant differences were found in the scores of the experimental and control subjects on either the retarded or the low-average level. Report card averages did not indicate superiority of the experimental groups over the control groups.

48. Champa, V. Anthony. "Television: Its Effectiveness in Ninth-Grade Science Teaching," *AV Communication Review*, VI (1958), 200-203.

The investigation was planned to explore the potential of television in helping ninth-grade pupils to learn more science with a view to making a career in the field and to determine the effectiveness of learning in face-to-face, instructional television, and film presentations. The pupils were divided into three groups. The analysis of variance indicated no significant differences in achievement scores among the three groups, although the boys in each group had higher scores than the girls.

49. Claye, Clifton M. "Lola Gets What Lola Wants from Supervision," *Journal of Educational Research*, LVI, No. 7 (March, 1963), 358-361.

This study involved 79 teachers enrolled in graduate school at Texas Southern University. Subjects responded to a questionnaire designed to find the kinds of services desired by teachers and the extent to which such services are received. Findings suggest that teachers want supervision from principals and from supervisors, but, in these teachers' opinion, principals do not supervise adequately.

50. Clements, Barton E. "Transitional Adolescents, Anxiety, and Group Counseling" *Personnel and Guidance Journal*, XLV, No. 1 (September, 1966), 67-71.

The subjects were 180 students randomly selected from the college-bound seniors in Mesa High School, Mesa, Arizona. The experimental groups exhibited significantly less anxiety concerning self both prior to and subsequent to college entrance as measured by the Index of Adjustment and Values. A comparison of the means scores on the Self-Concept Inventory and the Index of Adjustment and Values was made between the two groups to determine the effect of the counselor variable. No significant differences were found.

51. Coffield, William H. "Effects of Non-Promotion on Educational Achievement in the Elementary School," *Journal of Educational Psychology*, XLVIII (April, 1956), 235-250.

One hundred and forty-seven pupils who had experienced failure in one of the grades from three through six were studied. Failed pupils typically gained only six months during the repeated year and still failed to achieve the grade norm. The educational progress of failed pupils during the next two years was not significantly greater than that made by promoted matches during the single year spent in the next higher grade.

52. Cogan, Morris L. "Theory and Design of a Study of Teacher-Pupil Interaction" *Harvard Educational Review*, XXVI, No. 4 (Fall, 1956), 315-342.

This research was based upon data collected from administrators, teachers, and 987 eighth-grade pupils in five public junior high schools in two New England communities. In the individual pupil's perception, the teacher's conjunctive and inclusive behaviors were each positively related to the pupil's scores on required and self-initiated work. The trait of inclusiveness for all teachers was positively related to average required work scores and to average self-initiated work scores.

53. Condra, James Bruce. "A Study of the Effects of Frequency of Language Lab Experience and the Opportunity for Independent Study on Achievement in First-Year Spanish," *Dissertation Abstracts,* XXVI (1966), 5907.

Sixty students in first-year Spanish at an Alabama high school were used in the study. There was no statistically significant difference in the achievement of listening skills or of speaking skills. Laboratory sessions appeared to produce greater achievement of speaking skills if no opportunity for independent study was provided.

54. Coon, Lewis Hubert. "Study Group Mathematics as a Factor Influencing Success in Freshman Calculus," *Dissertation Abstracts*, XXV (1964), 4475.

   Which of two different high school preparatory curricula for college mathematics provided the better preparation for a first course in freshman calculus? A conventional group of 122 students and an SMSG group of 60 students were used. A significant difference favored the conventional group on the outdoor interest section of the Kuder Preference Record. The differences were due to continued mathematical maturity based on different high school preparation and not to learning in calculus.

55. Corwin, Ronald G. "Initiative and Compliance in Public Education," *Sociology of Education*, XXXVIII (Summer, 1965), 310-331.

   Using the Professional and Employee Role Conception Scale and another scale developed to estimate the tendency of teachers to use "initiative" or to show "compliance" to the administration, 257 subjects representing six schools in three different states were studied. It was found that professionalism is a militant process. While it cannot be said that militant teachers in the sample were necessarily professionally-oriented, the more professional teachers were militant.

56. Cousins, Jack E. "The Development of Reflective Thinking in an Eighth-Grade Social Studies Class," *Bulletin of the School of Education*, Indiana University, XXXIX (May, 1963), 36-58.

   This study described the development of reflective thinking skills in an eighth-grade social studies class. Pupils in the study group made significant gain in the accumulation of factual information pertinent to the social studies.

57. Cowan, Paul Jackson. "Development of New Autoinstructional Materials and an Analysis of Their Effectiveness in

Teaching Modern Physics in the Small High School," *Dissertation Abstracts*, XXV (1964), 2879.

> The sample consisted of 48 students from three Texas high schools who studied PSSC physics under the direction and guidance of a qualified physics teacher who was present with them in the classroom. Results of regressing reading ability scores and science background scores on achievement scores indicated that achievement on the PSSC achievements test 1 through 5 did not depend upon which of the two teaching methods was used by the students to study physics.

58. Cox, C. Benjamin. "A Description and Appraisal of a Reflective Method of Teaching United States History," *Bulletin of the School of Education*, Indiana University, XXXIX (May, 1963).

> This study proposed to determine the results of a reflective method of teaching a high school course in United States history in terms of critical thinking and achievement. The findings of the post-test failed to provide evidence that the reflective method of teaching resulted in increased skill in critical thinking. There were equal gains for both groups in the acquisition of facts, considering the length of the study.

59. Crumb, Glenn Howard. "A Study of Understanding Science Developed in High School Physics," *Dissertation Abstracts*, XXVI (1965), 1506.

> In a study population of 1,275 students from 29 high schools in Iowa, Kansas, Missouri, and Nebraska, a non-statistical analysis of teacher methods following class observations and interviews revealed differences in patterns of methods used by teachers whose classes showed highest and lowest mean gain in understanding science over the first-semester period.

60. Cyphert, Frederick R. "Current Practice in the Use of the Library in Selected Junior High Schools in Pennsylvania," *Dissertation Abstracts*, XVIII (1958), 162.

> A total of 73 usable replies were received from librarians in three-year junior high schools enrolling 500-1,000 students. All schools offered some type of pre-planned library instruction. Nearly 75 per cent

gave independently organized instruction and 70 per cent included integrated library instruction in the program of studies. Passive devices outranked active publicity techniques of the librarians. Most librarians were certified and devoted full time to the library.

61. Dandes, Herbert M. "Psychological Health and Teaching Effectiveness," *Journal of Teacher Education*, XVII (Spring, 1966), 301-305.

This study attempted to investigate the relationship between psychological health and the attitudes and values of teachers related to effective teaching. The study involved 128 teachers in central New York State. An inventory for measuring self-actualization, the Minnesota Teacher Attitude Inventory, the California F-Scale, and the Dogmatism Scale were used. There was a significant relationship between measured psychological health and the specified attitudes and values of teachers. The greater the psychological health, the greater the possession of attitudes and values characteristic of effective teaching.

62. Davis, Edward A. "A Study of Objective Differences Existing Between Small- and Large-Union High Schools in North Carolina," *Dissertation Abstracts,* XIX (1958), 1266.

One small high school (less than 10 teachers) and one large high school (17-39 teachers) were selected from each of thirteen North Carolina counties. Teacher-pupil ratios were slightly smaller in the smaller high schools. The class loads were greater in the smaller high schools. Professional quality of the staff was higher in the larger schools. Plant sites of the larger schools were superior in size, beauty, and development. The curricula of the larger schools were superior and they offered more co-curricular activities as well.

63. Day, William W. "Physics and Critical Thinking: An Experimental Evaluation of PSSC and Traditional Physics in Six Areas of Critical Thinking While Controlling for Intelligence, Achievement, Course Background, and Mobility by Analysis of Covariance," *Dissertation Abstracts*, XXV (1965), 4197.

One thousand and fifty-six students took six critical-thinking examinations in thirteen Colorado high schools.

The PSSC students had a negative attitude toward the course as compared to the non-PSSC students. The non-PSSC students were not only more positive in attitude toward their course, but were also more positive in the areas of interest in science and science activities.

64. Dean, Stuart E. "Pass or Fail? A Study of Promotion Policy," *Elementary School Journal*, LXI (November, 1960), 86-90.

The United States Office of Education made a comprehensive survey of the policies of public elementary schools with regard to promotion in which 4,284 urban places were polled. The national summary showed that 71 per cent of the urban places reported promotion practices based on academic progress. Academic achievement was the controlling factor in the promotion of elementary school children.

65. DeGraff, Homer R. "A Unit of Original Mathematics Investigation in Grade 9," *The Mathematics Teacher*, LV (January, 1962), 34-38.

This study was undertaken to determine if the Madison Project approach to teaching algebra and coordinate geometry by experiment and observation rather than by exposition could be used effectively on a class of ninth-graders. It was found that the Madison Project system of experimental learning resulted in work being done more accurately and with greater comprehension.

66. Deitz, James Emery. "Economic Understanding of Senior Students in Selected California High Schools," *Dissertation Abstracts*, XXIV (March, 1964), 3562-3563.

Nineteen schools from California were stratified on the basis of size and tests were administered to 3,908 seniors. There was need for greater emphasis on economic instruction. It was found that increased effectiveness in economic instruction in California high schools was needed with particular emphasis on added economic instruction in business courses.

67. Dempsey, Richard Allen. "An Analysis of Teachers' Expressed Judgments of Barriers to Curriculum Change in Relation to the Factor of Individual Readiness to Change," *Dissertation Abstracts*, XXIV (1963), 3225-3226.

Using 400 teachers, Dempsey administered a questionnaire containing statements thought to be rather universal concerns of teachers about obstacles which prevent them from carrying out curriculum changes. These statements were categorized into "internal barriers to change" and "external barriers to change." He found that younger teachers, male teachers, secondary teachers, and teachers with master's degrees perceived fewer barriers than did others.

68. Dolan, G. Keith. "Effects of Individual Counseling on Selected Test Scores for Delayed Readers," *Personnel and Guidance Journal*, XLII, No. 9 (May, 1964), 914-919.

    A study was made to determine the expressed attitudes of delayed readers in junior high school and, through a program of clinical counseling, to ascertain if (1) significant growth changes could be developed in these subjects; (2) these changes would alter stated and observed attitudes toward reading; (3) their reading abilities, as measured by standardized reading tests, would improve. A modified non-directive therapy approach was used. Ten subjects were enrolled in a formal reading program. Significant differences were obtained in reading achievement scores between students who had been individually counseled and those who had not.

69. Donelly, Edward Joseph. "Organization and Administration of Instructional Materials Centers in Selected High Schools," *Dissertation Abstracts*, XXVI, 5811.

    Literature was surveyed for historical development, the educational philosophy, most promising practices, and significant problems. All the selected centers were library centered, and (1) with few exceptions the centers did not fulfill ALA quantitative standards for (a) professional staff, (b) clerical staff, (c) books and periodicals available; (2) teachers generally rated status of professional staff members of the center lower than the directors; (3) centers were used more often by (a) teachers with more experience and advanced degrees and (b) teachers of social studies, science, and English.

70. Drexler, Henry Edward. "A Comparison of the Development of Critical Thinking in BSCS Biology of Ninth- and Tenth-Grade Students at Pius XI High School, Milwaukee,

Wisconsin." Unpublished master's thesis, Department of Education, The Ohio State University, Columbus, Ohio, 1964.

This study was designed to make a comparison of the development of critical thinking of ninth- and tenth-grade students in BSCS biology at Pius XI High School, Milwaukee, Wisconsin. Ninth-grade students developed the ability to think critically to a degree similar to that of tenth-grade students.

71. Driscoll, John P. "Can Television Improve College Teaching?" *NAEB Journal*, XVIII (March, 1956), 16-20.

This study involved a control group of 146 students composed of five separate classes at Pennsylvania State University taught by conventional non-visual methods, and an experimental group of approximately the same size. The television group did not achieve significantly more factual learning than did the non-television group.

72. Dyer-Bennett, John, William R. Fuller, Warren F. Seibert, and Merrill E. Shanks. "Teaching Calculus by Closed-Circuit Television," *American Mathematical Monthly*, LXIII (July, 1958), 430-439.

The main problem studied was the comparative effectiveness of televised and conventional first-semester calculus instruction. Sixty-one pairs of matched students served as subjects for the comparison of achievement of students in the experimental and control groups. Student achievement was very nearly the same for conventional and television-taught students. No statistical difference was found when comparing the total semester's performance of these groups.

73. Ebert, Mary Gertrude. "An Analysis of Certain Characteristics of Secondary School Teachers Rated as Most Approachable and Least Approachable by Secondary School School Students," *Dissertation Abstracts*, XXVII (1965), 4327-4328.

The study involved 66 secondary school teachers and 1,131 secondary school students in two Oregon public high schools. Students identified teachers as most approachable and least approachable for vocational and personal problems. Students preferred to discuss problems with teachers of the same sex. Source of acquaintance with teachers was more likely to be "known by reputation only" for least approachable than for most approachable teachers. More lower socio-economic class than higher socio-economic class boys chose industrial-arts teachers as most approachable.

74. Eigen, Lewis D. "High School Student Reactions to Programmed Instruction," *Phi Delta Kappan,* XLIV (March, 1963), 282-285.

The subjects were 72 male students enrolled at the Collegiate School, New York City. Students' attitudes toward programmed instruction were little different from their attitudes toward other types of instructional techniques. Also, the students' total attitude toward the method of learning seemed to have no relationship to what they had learned by that method.

75. Elsmere, Robert T. "An Experimental Study Utilizing the Problem-Solving Approach in Teaching United States History," *Bulletin of the School of Education,* Indiana University, XXXIX (May, 1963), 114-134.

In this study, the subjects were selected from high school juniors enrolled at Elmhurst High School, Fort Wayne, Indiana. Only those juniors who had been enrolled previously in a full year of general history were considered. It was found that a problem-solving approach to teaching United States history produced significantly greater pupil achievement than did a traditional approach.

76. Enzmann, Arthur Milton. "An Evaluation of the Science and Arts Curriculum For Selected Students of High Ability at Cass Technical High School, Detroit, Michigan." *Dissertation Abstracts,* XXII (1962), 3484.

A group of 206 seniors was included. There were significant differences in five comparisons out of thirty-eight regarding academic achievement. Three of the comparisons differed significantly in favor of the experimental groups. There was no consistent superiority of the experimental group over the control group.

77. Farley, Eugene S., *et al.* "Factors Relating to the Grade Progress of Pupils," *Elementary School Journal,* XXXIV (November, 1933), 186-193.

All twelve-year pupils in two Newark schools were examined to determine their mental ability, achievement, health, school attendance, social status, and character traits. The study showed a definite relationship between grade progress of pupils and ability and achievement. There was no significant relationship between grade placement and health or socio-economic status.

78. Farley, John J. "Book Censorship in the Senior High School Libraries of Nassau County, New York," *Dissertation Abstracts,* XXV (1965), 5948-49.

This study attempted to discover the nature of book censorship as performed in the senior high schools' libraries of Nassau County, New York, to identify the sources of this censorship, and to ascertain its rationale. Fifty-four head librarians in senior high schools participated. All librarians performed some book censorship on occasion; about 30 per cent rarely censored; less than 10 per cent usually or habitually censored; more than 60 per cent fell in a middle ground. All librarians censored novels which treated sex too explicitly, some types of sex-education books, and some books dealing with religion. A majority censored art books with pictures of nudes, and some books on politics, especially with extreme or one-sided treatment of communism or race.

79. Ferris, Frederick L., Jr. "An Achievement Test Report," *Progress Report.* Cambridge: Educational Services, Inc., 1959.

The 278 schools participating in the PSSC program were asked to administer the School and College Ability Test (SCAT). The course was well within the capabilities of the great majority of United States high school physics students, and experience with it was also highly profitable to a sizable percentage of relatively low-aptitude students.

80. Fincher, Glen E. and H. T. Fillmer. "Programmed Instruction in Elementary Arithmetic," *The Arithmetic Teacher,* XII (Janurary, 1965), 19-23.

Ten classes involving 309 fifth-grade students in three schools were assigned at random to experimental and control treatments. Programmed textbooks used were found to be more effective than the conventional classroom approach to the study of addition and subtraction of fractions, and to be as effective as the conventional classroom approach in the retention of acquired knowledge on the addition and subtraction of fractions. Subjects with higher grade levels of arithmetic skills made greater gains than those with lower grade levels of arithmetic skills.

81. Fisk, W. W. "The Effectiveness of Ability Grouping in Seventh-Grade Core Classes." Unpublished Ed. D. dissertation, University of Kansas, 1962.

For this study, seventh-grade pupils at Olathe Junior High School in Kansas were ranked according to ability to do academic work. Control and experimental groups were formed. It was found that main effects of the experimental factor were not significant in any measured area of skill development. The average effect of the experimental factor was not significant in the areas of peer behavior, learning needs, and teacher-pupil relationships.

82. Flanders, N. A. "Personal-Social Anxiety as a Factor in Experimental Learning Situations," *Journal of Educational Research,* XLV (October, 1951), 100-110.

With large quantities of data per subject, a total of seven subjects was used. Student behavior associated with interpersonal anxiety took priority over behavior oriented toward the achievement problem. Teacher behavior characterized as acceptant, problem-oriented, evaluative, or critical by way of public criteria, and, in general, supportive, elicited behaviors of problem orientation and decreased interpersonal anxiety, integration, and even emotional readjustment.

83. Flanders, N. A. "Teacher Influence, Pupil Attitudes, and Achievement," *U.S. Office of Education, Department of Health, Education and Welfare. Cooperative Research Project No. 397,* University of Minnesota, November, 1960.

The data here were obtained in the Minneapolis and St. Paul public schools and from research done in Wellington, New Zealand. The project included 16 mathematics and 16 social studies teachers who taught a two-week unit of study. The students who achieved the most and had significantly higher scores on the attitude instrument were in classes exposed to flexible patterns of teacher influence.

84. Flanders, Ned A. "Using Interaction Analysis in the In-Service Training of Teachers, " *Journal of Experimental Education,* XXX (June, 1962), 313-316.

This study involved a nine-week in-service training program in which 55 teachers participated. They were mostly from two suburban junior high schools near Minneapolis. The teachers made changes in their pattern of spontaneous verbal behavior that were statistically significant and in a direction consistent with the objectives of the in-service training.

85. French, J. W. "Evidence from School Records on the Affectiveness of Ability Grouping," *Journal of Educational Research,* LIV (November, 1960), 83-91.

For this study, data from the files of the James Monroe High School in New York City, and from the Naval Training Centers at Bainbridge and Norfolk were used. It was found that in the analysis of both Navy and civilian data, there was no relationship between achievement and homogeneity of ability within classes.

86. French, Lillian A. "A Study of the Progress Made By Twenty-Four Retarded Readers in an Improvement Program," *Dissertation Abstracts,* XVI (1956), 115.

This study was conducted to assess the effects of a one-year program of remediation in the area of reading. The 24 subjects were from the fifth through the eighth grades of the public schools in Maricopa, California. Significant gains were made in silent reading, oral reading, and in spelling.

87. Friebel, Allen Cahoun. "A Comparative Study of Achievement and Understanding of Measurment among Students Enrolled in Traditional and Modern School Mathematics Programs, *Dissertation Abstracts,* XXVI (1965), 903-904.

A sample of 185 seventh-grade pupils was drawn for random assignment to experimental SMSG and control (traditional) groups. Significant differences in arithmetic reasoning and in learnings associated with measurement were found favoring the SMSG instructional group. No differences were found in total achievement or in arithmetic fundamentals and no significant differences were found between the high- and low-intelligence groups.

88. Friedman, Robert. "A Comparison of Two Instructional Programs for Severely Retarded Readers at the Junior High School Level," *Dissertation Abstracts,* XXV (1965), 5110-5111.

The sample consisted of 116 students, retarded in reading at least one and one-half years, enrolled in two seventh-grade, two eighth-grade, and two ninth-grade remedial reading classes. Intraprogram comparisons of the effect of socioeconomic status revealed no significant differences. The reading-for-pleasure program and the skill-oriented program were equally effective in producing reading improvement.

89. Fry, Edward B. "Teaching Machines: An Investigation of Constructed versus Multiple-Choice Methods of Response," *Automated Teaching Bulletin,* I (1959), 11-12.

This study attempted to determine whether a constructed or a multiple-choice response was the most efficient for teaching a list of Spanish words and phrases to 153 ninth-grade beginning students of Spanish. Constructed training responses resulted in more learning than did multiple-choice responses when the criterion of learning was recall.

90. Frye, Charles H. "Group-vs-Individual Pacing in Programmed Instruction," *AV Communication Review,* II (July-August, 1963), 124-30.

Four groups of high school freshmen comprised the sample. All were beginning a course in algebra. The study was designed to investigate some of the conditions under which the adaptation of self-instructional techniques to a group setting were most feasible. This suggested the efficiency potential that group-pacing techniques with programmed materials have in the context of a graded school system.

91. Fulmer, Earl Ray. An Evaluation of High School Honors Programs in Preparing Students for College. *Dissertation Abstracts,* XXIV (1963), 571.

The experimental group involved 96 pupils who had participated in programs involving ability grouping, acceleration, or college courses in high school. The control group was composed of 56 students who had not participated in such programs. Differences favored the experimental group, but the only differences that were significant were in grade-point averages and numbers of honors courses taken during the first year of college.

92. Gagné, Robert M. and Walter, Dick. "Learning Measures in a Self-Instructional Program in Solving Equations," *Psychological Reports,* X (1962), 131-146.

Subjects were 52 seventh-grade mathematics students from Valley Road School, Princeton, New Jersey. The students were from the "middle-ability" mathematics group. All students felt that they had learned something, and most felt that they would remember at least a little of the material.

93. Garside, Leonard J. "A Comparison of the Effectiveness of Two Methods of Instruction in High School Physics as Measured by Levels of Achievement of Students of High and Low Intelligence," *Dissertation Abstracts,* XX (1959), 2172-2173.

Sixty Wisconsin school groups were randomly selected to participate. The level of achievement and retention in physics of high and low intelligence respectively in the experimental group was not significantly different from that of comparable students in the control group. There was no significant difference in the level of achievement between the experimental group and the control group.

94. Georgiades, William and Joan Bjelke. "Evaluation of English Achievement in a Ninth-Grade, Three-Period, Team-teaching Project," *California Journal of Education Research,* (May, 1966), 100-112.

At Charter Oak High School, 106 ninth-grade students were involved in this study. Analysis revealed significant differences in average scores for the teacher-made test and for the Reading Comprehension section of the California Reading Test. There was no difference with respect to the Reading Vocabulary section. The statistically significant difference in the unadjusted and adjusted means favored the experimental group.

Appendix A

95. Gibson, R. E. "Final Report on the Westside High School Teaching by Tape Project," *National Association of Secondary School Principals Bulletin,* XLIV (January, 1960), 56-62.

Fifteen seventh-grade classes were taught spelling and penmanship in a single twenty-minute broadcast by a single tape recorder plugged into a hi-fidelity PA system, and a central group was taught the same material in a conventional manner by a regular teacher. The difference between means, after adjustment, was highly significant in favor of the tape plus supplemental-list experimental group.

96. Gibson, Robert L. "Teacher Opinions of High School Guidance Programs," *Personnel and Guidance Journal,* XLIV, No. 4 (December, 1965), 416-422.

This study attempted to study the school guidance program from the viewpoint of the classroom teacher. Subjects were 208 secondary school teachers from 18 schools in Ohio, Michigan, West Virginia, and Indiana. Teachers recognized counseling as the heart of the school guidance program and appeared to confer regularly with counselors regarding student problems; they were not hesitant to use counselors for referral purposes. Not a single teacher had been involved in inservice training regarding theories of vocational choice. Most teachers felt the guidance worker should identify pupil interest but not be necessarily involved in group activities. Teachers did not understand the counseling process and the principle of confidentiality.

97. Glad, Joan Rogers Bourne. "Evaluation of the Remedial Reading Program in Utah Public Schools," *Dissertation Abstracts,* XXVI (1966), 5864.

Subjects were 1,512 pupils from grades three through twelve, enrolled in remedial classes at the beginning and end of the remedial year. Average gain in oral reading was 1.57 grades which was significant at the .01 level of confidence. Correlation of the verbal ability scores with reading gains of pupils was significant at the .05 level.

98. Glanz, Edward, V. F. Calia and Gene Smith. "Scholastic Growth in a Program Using the Team Approach," *Journal of Educational Research,* LVII (March, 1964), 386-387.

This study attempted to provide an objective indication of the success of the team approach at the College of Basic Studies Level of Boston University. Scholastic growth was evaluated in terms of change of scores on the Graduate Record Examination. As freshman, the team group was below the national average on the GRE, but at the end of the sophomore year, they were above the national average. Correlations between pre-scores and growth scores were found to be very low for all three areas tested.

99. Glennon, Vincent J. "A Study in Needed Redirection in the Preparation of Teachers of Arithmetic," *The Mathematics Teacher,* XLII (December, 1949), 389-396.

For this study, 144 teachers-college freshmen, 172 teachers-college seniors, and 160 inservice teachers were tested with an 80-item test of mathematics understanding. The inservice teachers did not grow in understanding of the subject-matter of arithmetic by taking a graduate course in the psychology and teaching of arithmetic, nor did they grow in understanding of the subject matter of arithmetic as a result of experience in teaching arithmetic over a period of one or more years.

100. Gold, Joy Rochell. "The Effect of Administrative Atmosphere on the Role of the School Teacher," *Dissertation Abstracts,* XXVI (1965), 1201.

A total of 1,250 white elementary school teachers participated. Each school was identified as democratic, autocratic, medium, or having no consensus, on the basis of the teachers' average score on a scale measuring their perception of the principal's behavior. Democratic principals produced teachers with higher job satisfaction, higher career satisfaction, less tendency to form cliques, higher satisfaction with pupils and their parents. There seemed to be no relationship between the administrative behavior of the principal and the teachers' feelings toward other teachers in the schools.

101. Goldberg, Miriam L., A. H. Passow, and Joseph Justman. *The Effects of Ability Grouping.* New York: Teachers College Press, 1966, p. 254.

This study involved 2,200 students in 86 elementary classes over a period of two years. Assessments included pre- and post-tests in academic achievement interests, attitudes toward school, attitudes toward self, attitudes toward more and less able pupils, and teacher appraisal. The general conclusion was that narrowing the ability range on the basis of some measure of general aptitude produces little positive change in the academic achievement of pupils at any ability level. There was no support for negative effects in other areas.

102. Goodlad, John I. "Some Effects of Promotion and Non-Promotion upon the Social and Personal Adjustment of Children," *Journal of Experimental Education,* XXII (June, 1954), 301-327.

Six elementary schools from which non-promoted children were to be chosen were selected. Five elementary schools from which the promoted children were to be chosen were then selected. The final groups were equated. There were differences in both social adjustment and personal adjustment between repeating and non-repeating school children. Differences in the area of peer group relationships favored the promoted group.

103. Goodman, Thomas L. "Instructional Programs in Secondary Schools Serving Contrasting Socio-Economic Areas in Large Cities," *Dissertation Abstracts,* XXVI (1966), 3699.

Seven large-city school systems in the midwestern United States cooperated in the study by providing four schools each for study and visitation. Each city system selected schools "typical" of those serving depressed and priviledged socio-economic areas of the city. General findings revealed that there was little difference in the curriculum of the schools. The greatest difference found was in the human dimension of the program. The instructional staffs of the more privileged area schools were more stable, had more educational preparation, and had more professional experience than their depressed area counterparts.

104. Gottschulk, Gunther H. "Closed Circuit Television in Second Semester College German," *Modern Language Journal,* XLIX (February, 1965), 86-91.

This study investigated the possible advantages of presenting fundamental foreign language materials to large groups of college students by means of television. Seventy-six per cent of the students felt they were learning more in the TV course, and 89 per cent realized that television instruction put more responsibility on the shoulders of the student. The television class outperformed the non-television class in aural comprehension and in translation of English sentences into German.

105. Gragg, Irene A. "A Reading Improvement Program for a Special Ninth-Grade English Class." Unpublished master's thesis, The Ohio State University, 1956.

Seventy-three students participated. The results indicated a median progress of 1.1 years in a seven and one-half month interval. This progress had been made possible by providing a well-balanced, free-reading program in combination with the reading-skills program.

106. Grassell, Edward Milton. "An Evaluation of Educational Films in the Teaching of High School Physics in Oregon," *Dissertation Abstracts,* XXI (1960), 820-821.

There were 471 students involved. High school physics courses taught primarily with the White Physics Films were as effective as courses taught in the more traditional lecture-demonstration manner. The White Physics Film Series contained presentations and demonstrations that time and money limitations did not permit in the more typical classroom situation.

107. Grassmeyer, Donald Leroy. "Organization and Administration of Instructional Materials Centers in Selected Junior High Schools," *Dissertation Abstracts,* XXVII (1966), 68-69.

Forty schools in 14 states were used in this study. Teachers who made extensive use of the centers were identified by directors and their responses were solicited. The centers tended to be library centered, but teachers and directors recognized the need and were attempting to develop and implement the audio-visual aspect. With few exceptions, the centers did not fulfill standards of AASL or guidelines of DAVI for personnel, equipment, and materials. Teachers with less than 10 years experience and under 39 years of age used the centers most extensively.

108. Grobman, Hulda. "High School Biology, On What Level Does It Belong?" *The Clearing House,* XXXVIII, No. 8 (April, 1964), 498-499.

Appendix A

Thirty-six ninth-grade teachers used experimental editions of the BSCS materials with average and above-average students. Above-average ninth-graders, did a highly satisfactory job with all of the three versions. Average and below-average students appeared to be penalized by taking biology in the ninth grade. It was concluded that if the school district decided to offer biology at both the senior and junior high levels, the junior high classes should be restricted to the most able students.

109. Grobman, Hulda. "Student Performance in New High School Biology Programs," *Science,* CXLIII, No. 3603 (January 17, 1964), 265-266.

Achievement of BSCS students on the BSCS Comprehensive Examination was significantly higher than that of the tenth-grade students in the control group. The achievement of the control group was significantly higher on the Cooperative Test than that of the BSCS students. On the BSCS Impact, the results were not definitive. No significant relationship was found between achievement and type of school (urban, rural), size of school, length of class period or number of periods per week, expenditure per pupil, or characteristics of the teacher (age, experience, etc.).

110. Grobman, Hulda. "Who is the 'Slow Learner' in Biology?" *Fast Journal* (Florida Association of Science Teachers), XX (April-May, 1964), 20-22.

BSCS Comprehensive Final Tests were administered. Students at or above the 50th percentile were able to handle the regular BSCS material. Schools were not assigning students to slow-learner classes based on student ability as measured by reading or general ability tests. Some students between the 40th and 50th percentile were able to handle the regular materials.

111. Groff, Frank H. "Effects on Academic Achievement of Excusing Elementary School Pupils from Classes to Study Instrumental Music," *Dissertation Abstracts,* XXV (March, 1965), 5014-5015.

This study was limited to sixth-grade children in 15 elementary schools of West Hartford, Connecticut. Pupils were divided into two groups for comparison: (1) those who were at the time of the study taking instrumental music lessons in school and were being excused from classes to do so, and (2) those pupils who were not taking instrumental music lessons in school. There was no significant difference in academic achievement of the two groups. Sixth-grade pupils who were excused from classes in this experiment to take instrumental music lessons once or twice per week for limited periods did not suffer any loss of academic achievement as measured by the Iowa Tests of Basic Skills.

112. Gropper, George L. and Arthur A. Lumsdaine. "An Experimental Comparison of a Conventional TV Lesson with a Programmed TV Lesson Requiring Active Student Response," *Studies in Televised Instruction,* Report No. 2, Metropolitan Pittsburgh Educational Television Station, WQED-WQEX and American Institute for Research, 1961.

There were 140 subjects who were junior high students. The experimental group scored higher than the control group on five tests. Two of the five comparisons were statistically significant, and a third was significant for some of the schools in the sample.

113. Gropper, George L. and Arthur A. Lumsdaine, "An Investigation of the Role of Selected Variables in Programmed TV Instruction," *Studies in Televised Instruction,* Report No. 4, Metropolitan Pittsburgh Educational TV Stations, WQED and WQEX and American Institute for Research, 1961.

Subjects for this study were 784 junior high school science students and it consisted of four experiments. There were no significant differences found in any of the four comparisons. Active competition, intermittent feedback, written responses, and oral responses have little if any effect on the effectiveness of educational television.

114. Grotberg, Edity. "The Washington Report in Action," *Education,* LXXXV (April, 1965), 490-494.

This study attempted to determine if a classroom teacher, using available selected materials and with special assistance from a supervisor, could bring about significant gains in reading for ninth-grade disadvantaged Negro boys. The mean gain for the total reading scores was 1.5 years, in 12 weeks.

Appendix A 121

115. Grote, Charles Nelson. "A Comparison of the Relative Effectiveness of Direct-Detailed and Directed Discovery Methods of Teaching Selected Principles of Mechanics in the Area of Physics," *Dissertation Abstracts,* XXI, 3016-3017.

> The ability levels were estimated on the basis of outside criteria. There was a single control group. Subjects were selected at random from a single eighth-grade class in a suburban junior high school. The group instructed by the direct-detailed method was superior to the directed discovery group as measured by the first initial learning test. There was no difference between these groups when measured for initial learning following the second lesson, or for retention and transfer at one and six weeks. The relative effect of methods, as well as certain treatment sequences, was dependent in part, upon the sex and/or ability of the subject.

116. Grubb, Betty Sayre. "A Proposal for Emphasizing Modern Mathematics in Elementary Algebra," United States Office of Education, Bulletin, 1960.

> This study involved 21 students in the tenth grade or higher and was undertaken to prepare, teach, and evaluate materials correlated with present-day textbooks in elementary algebra so as to emphasize modern concepts. The gains in scores on the test were extensive among the 17 students who finished the course. Another outcome was greater pupil sensitivity to reasonable answers and possible answers.

117. Guilford, J. P., Ralph Hoepfner, and Hugh Peterson. "Predicting Achievement in Ninth-Grade Mathematics from Measures of Intellectual-Aptitude Factors," *Educational and Psychological Measurement,* XXV (Autumn, 1965), 659-682.

> An entire ninth-grade class, which numbered approximately 600, participated. Batteries of factor scores were better predictors of achievement than two of the standard test combinations, especially in the prediction of achievement in algebra. Of the factors that were relevant to discrimination between the two kinds of students (general mathematics and algebra), most of them were also relevant for prediction within courses of either kind or both.

118. Halliwell, Joseph W. "A Comparison of Pupil Achievement

in Graded and Nongraded Primary Classrooms," *Journal of Experimental Education,* XXXII (Fall, 1963), 59-64.

This study attempted to determine whether a nongraded pattern of organization in reading and spelling in the primary grades resulted in improved academic achievement. The findings at the first-grade level reflected a clear-cut superiority for the nongraded pupils. At the second- and third-grade levels, findings favored the nongraded pupils, but none of the differences were significant.

119. Hamilton, Mary Una. "An Experiment in the Teaching of Algebra I from the Contemporary Point of View," United States Office of Education, Bulletin 1963, No. 12, p. 42.

In this study, students of contemporary Algebra I were compared with students of traditional Algebra I by means of pre-tests and post-tests. There was increased enthusiasm of students in the contemporary section, but their achievement was not better than that of students in the traditional section.

120. Harous, Delbert, John L. Hayman, and James Johnson. "Programming Instruction in Elementary Spanish," *Phi Delta Kappan,* XLIV (March, 1963), 269-272.

Sixth-grade pupils in Denver schools were randomly divided into two groups. Each group consisted of approximately 90 classes with 3,000 pupils. It was concluded that with proper conditions and at least with rather mechanical learning, automated instruction could have been as effective as the more tradition-directed method. The training and experience of the classroom teachers had an effect on the amount pupils learned from automated instruction.

121. Hart, Richard H. "The Nongraded Primary School and Arithmetic," *The Arithmetic Teacher,* IX (March, 1962), 130-133.

A matched-pair study was conducted comparing the arithmetic achievement of pupils in graded classrooms with pupils in the nongraded primary school. Twenty-six per cent of the graded group fell below grade level, while 14 per cent of the experimental or nongraded group received a score below grade level.

Appendix A

122. Hayman, John L., Jr. and James T. Johnson, Jr. "Exact -vs- Varied Repetition in Educational Television," *AV Communication Review,* II (July-August, 1963), 96-103.

> How much will a second viewing of a TV lesson increase learning? This study involved 192 fifth-grade Spanish classes and approximately 6,000 pupils. Exact repetition significantly increased learning when there was no other practice. It was not as effective as teacher-directed classroom practice, however, and its ability to increase learning when added to classroom practice varied inversely with the training and experience of the classroom teacher.

123. Hemphill, John K. "Leader Behavior Associated with the Administrative Reputations of College Departments," *Journal of Educational Psychology* reprinted in *Leader Behavior: Its Description and Measurement.* Columbus, Ohio: Bureau of Business Research, 1957.

> This study was concerned with leadership and administration in 22 departments in a liberal arts college of a moderately large university. Older and more mature faculty members provided a larger portion of the "reputation" information than the younger or new members of the faculty. A department's "reputation" for being well administered was related to the leadership behavior of the department chairman as this behavior was described by department members. Departments with good administration had chairmen described as above average in both *consideration* and *initiating structure.* Larger departments tended to have better administrative reputations than small departments.

124. Henderson, Clara A. "An Evaluation of the Workshop Program for In-Service Teacher Education by the Ohio State Department of Education, 1944-1947." Unpublished doctoral dissertation, The Ohio State University, 1948.

> This study attempted to appraise the effectiveness of the workshop program directed by the Ohio State Department of Education for promoting the in-service growth of elementary school teachers in Ohio. There were 26 workshops involving over 1,600 teachers. Not one of the criteria developed was met adequately

and, in general, it was concluded that the workshops were not effective ventures in in-service education.

125. Hendrix, Oscar R. "The Effect of Special Advising on Achievement of Freshmen with Low Predicted Grades," *Personnel and Guidance Journal,* XLIV, No. 2 (October, 1965), 185-188.

The purpose of this study was to determine whether the achievement of University of Wyoming students with low predicted grades might be improved by special advising. There were 40 subjects. The experimental group achieved significantly better than the control groups in all subject fields. There was no substantial difference between the achievement of the sample of students attending a pre-college orientation conference and of those not attending.

126. Herminghous, Earl G. "Large Group Instruction by Television: An Experiment," *School Review,* LXV (1957), 119-133.

This study compared the achievement of students in ninth-grade general science and English who were taught solely by a competent television teacher with the achievement of students taught by regular teachers in conventional classroom settings. There were no significant differences in achievement, although students did not react favorably to the television teaching.

127. Hillson, Maurie, *et al.* "A Controlled Experiment Evaluating the Effects of a Nongraded Organization on Pupil Achievement," *Journal of Educational Research,* LVII (July, 1964), 548-560.

All first-grade students entering the Washington Elementary School were randomly assigned to either the experimental or control group. They remained in these groups for three years. The experimental group scored higher in the Lee Clark Reading list in 'word meaning and paragraph meaning.

128. Hipsher, Warren L. "Study of High School Physics Achievement," *The Science Teacher,* XXVIII (October, 1961), 36-38.

Two hundred and eight male seniors of Will Rogers High School, Tulsa, Oklahoma were included in this study. The groups had the same teacher, the same length of time, in the same classroom, and the same approximate class size. Traditional students did significantly better on the Cooperative Physics Test than the students taught high school physics using PSSC.

129. Hoban, Pierce F. and Barry McManus. "How to Nongrade a Small High School," *School Management,* IX, No. 9 (September, 1965), 79-81.

The experiment was undertaken in a 100-student senior high school in Tuxedo Park, New York. Both English and social studies were cycled because these subjects were not, in the main, sequential. By making careful use of tests, teacher recommendations, and student achievement every year, students were grouped accurately, according to needs. It was concluded that courses should not be cycled, however, unless many of the students are sophisticated enough and ambitious enough to make nongrading work.

130. Hopkins, Kenneth D. and D. Welty Lefever. "Comparative Learning and Retention of Conventional and Instructional TV Methods," *AV Communication Review,* XXIII (Spring, 1965), 28-37.

For this study, each of the 20 elementary schools in the Anaheim City school district were randomly assigned to one of three method groups, and the entire group of fourth-and fifth-grade pupils received instruction either conventionally or with one of the two ITV methods. Groups receiving the televised social studies instruction performed significantly better on the end-of-term examinations than did the control groups.

131. Houston, William Robert, Jr. "Selected Methods of In-Service Education and the Mathematics Achievement and Interest of Elementary School Pupils." Unpublished doctoral dissertation, University of Texas, 1961.

In addition to the independent variables of in-service presentation media, consultant service, and time, grade level and class achievement grouping were added. There was no significant difference in the methods of in-service education as reflected in the achievement and interest of the participating teachers' pupils.

132. Howell, Wallace J. "Influence of Curriculum Enrichment in High School Honors Group on College Board Examination Scores," *Journal on Educational Research,* LIX, No. 3 (November, 1965), 113-114.

There were 21 students in the control group and 28 in the experimental group. Grouping of gifted and talented students appeared to achieve desirable results. Grouping did not achieve significant differences in the area of mathematics.

133. Huettig, Alice and John M. Newell. "Attitudes Toward Introduction of Modern Mathematics Program by Teachers with Large and Small Number of Years Experience," *The Arithmetic Teacher,* XIII (February, 1966), 125-128.

One hundred and fifteen elementary teachers were given questionnaires designed to sample attitudes toward new mathematics programs. Teachers with less than ten years experience were more positive in their attitudes than those with more than ten years experience. No significant differences in reaction according to grade taught were shown. Teachers with no training in the new mathematics tended to have a negative attitude toward the program. Good training was essential for positive attitudes toward modern mathematics and it was concluded that teachers with no training should not teach it. A workshop was not sufficient training for teaching modern mathematics.

134. Hughes, Marie. "The Assessment of the Quality of Teaching: A Research Report," *U. S. Office of Education Cooperative Research Project No. 353,* University of Utah, 1959.

Forty-one teachers served as subjects. Only three teachers had all of their records with 20 or more of their teaching acts in the category of development of content. Seventy-four per cent of all records had 20 per cent or less of teaching acts falling in this category of exploration, amplification, utilization of children's questions and remarks, evaluation, and stimulation. In dealing with subject matter, little attention was given to children's exploratory remarks or their questions. The questions teachers used for structure were usually closed; that is, asked for one answer.

135. Hunt, Edward G. "Team Teaching in Junior High School Science and Social Studies," *Dissertation Abstracts,* XXIV (May, 1964), 4583.

Two groups of seventh-grade pupils totaling 150 at Gorton Junior High School, Warwick, Rhode Island were compared in terms of academic achievement and personality development. Academic achievement of pupils in junior high school science and social studies was neither improved nor impaired by team teaching, and team teaching methods did not make significant changes in the personality development of pupils.

136. Hunt, Ronald Leroy. "The Effects of the San Diego Community Educational Resources Project on the Teaching of Elementary Space Science," *Dissertation Abstracts,* XXV (1964), 1683.

The criterion to measure the success of the program was the assessment of changes in science achievement of fifth- and sixth grade students in two elementary school districts in San Diego County, California. Comparisons of student ability and achievement in science were made. It was felt that a community-wide communications system could be developed to reduce the time lag between the discovery of new scientific knowledge in the community and its availability to the teacher and learner in a form that would change student behavior. The simultaneous use of an inservice education program combined with instructional materials was an effective means for the communication of new knowledge to the student via the teacher.

137. Huntinger, Paul. "Effect of Systematic Horizontal-Ladder Exercises upon Upper Body Strength of Third-Grade Children," *Research Quarterly,* XXV (1955), 159-162.

There were two groups: the experimental group of 34 students and the control group of 32 students. These were Kansas City, Missouri third-grade children ranging in age from eight years to ten years eight months old. The total amount of time for physical education activities given to the experimental group was the same as that given to the control group. The experimental group made statistically significant gains in push-ups, pull-ups, pushing strength, and pulling strength. The hand-grip gains were not statistically significant because those particular muscle groups were not exercised actively.

138. Ikeda, Hiroshi. "A Factorial Study of the Relationship between Teacher-Held Objectives and Student Performance in UICSM High School Mathematics," *Dissertation Abstracts,* XXVI (1965), 2588.

A total of 154 ninth-grade pupils were pre-and-post-tested. The test booklets were sent to 105 teachers who taught UICSM mathematics for evaluation. The teachers were from 70 different schools in 19 states. In the case of student gains, no factor was significantly congruent with teacher ratings. However, mean gain scores showed a positive relationship with mean teacher ratings.

139. Jackson, Joseph. "Analysis of a Team Teaching and a Self-Contained Homeroom Experiment in Grades Five—Six" *Journal of Experimental Education,* XXXII (Summer, 1964), 317-331.

The team approach as applied in this study merged and divided two classrooms of students for teaching by a team of teachers. Pre-tests of achievement and mental ability provided data for the division of the groups. Significant differences in grade five occurred in reading achievement in the team-teaching group and grade five maintained a superior status in language and science. Significant differences occurred in grade six in work-study skills in the team approach. The maladjusted and the isolated seemed to face increased social disequilibrium under the team program.

140. Jacobs, James N. and Joan K. Bollenbacker. "Teaching Ninth-Grade Biology by Television," *AV Communication Review,* VIII (July-August, 1960), 176-191.

Four classes of four representative schools in Cincinnati were chosen for the experiment. Pupils with below-average ability tended to prefer TV while above-average students tended to favor conventional instruction. No significant differences between methods were noted in terms of the degree to which students thought they had learned biology. Both methods of instruction appeared to result in the same amount of time being spent studying biology. This was true for all levels of students.

141. Jacobs, James N., Althea Beery, and Judith Leinwold. "Evaluation of an Accelerated Arithmetic Program," *The Arithmetic Teacher,* XII (February, 1965), 113-119.

The Cincinnati Public Schools initiated a five-year experiment of arithmetic acceleration in selected schools in grades three through six. The plan was to provide a more challenging program of arithmetic instruction for capable pupils. Accelerates who pursued either the SMSG or the conventional program in seventh grade did better than the non-accelerates. The effects of acceleration in elementary school and the SMSG program in grade seven appeared to be additive in terms of increased achievement in both conventional and SMSG subject matter.

142. Jacobs, James N. and Joan K. Bollenbacher. "An Experimental Study of the Effectiveness of Television versus Classroom Instruction in Sixth-Grade Science in the Cincinnati Public Schools, 1956-57," *Journal of Educational Research,* LII (1958-1959), 184-189.

Twelve classes of sixth-grade science with 315 boys and girls located in 12 elementary schools were included in the experiments. The results did not consistently favor one group, since the television groups were seen to exceed the non-television groups at the "high" level while the reverse was true at the "low" level. At the "middle"-ability level, there was little difference between the mean scores.

143. Janes, Robert W. "Pre-existing Attitudes of College Students to Instructional Television," *AV Communication Review,* XII (Fall, 1964), 325-336.

About 400 students in a large midwestern university were involved in this study. Students high on a scale of "self-confidence" showed a preference or positive evaluation of televised lectures. The assumption of independence of intelligence scores and preference for television was not demonstrated. Grades received in the course had a direct effect on the evaluation of the course given by the student.

144. Jantzen, Victor W. "The Effectiveness of Television Teaching of American Government Compared with Regular Classes in Wichita High School South," *Dissertation Abstracts,* XXIV (September-October, 1963), 1029.

The subjects were 165 senior high school students regularly enrolled in American government. Television teaching did not prove to be superior when the overall achievement was compared with that of the regular classes taught by conventional instructional procedures. The conventional classroom method proved to be superior in the teaching of the two units on national government and local government.

145. Jensen, Lawrell, Wanda B. Riggle, Philip Merkley, and Rhoda Rudy. "Eighth-Grade Team Teaching at the Roosevelt Junior High School," *California Journal of Secondary Education,* XXXV, No. 4 (April, 1960), 236-243.

Eighth-grade students were divided into four relatively homogenous sections using the criteria of mental ability, scholastic achievement, and teacher evaluation. The combined experimental group achieved higher mean gain scores in the areas of history and language arts. One experimental group achieved significantly higher mean gain scores both in language arts and history. The two retarded groups showed results somewhat in reverse of the general trend. There was a significant correlation between IQ scores and gain scores. A sociometric device was administered which showed no statistically significant gains or losses.

146. Jessell, John C. and John W. M. Rothney. "The Effectiveness of Parent-Counselor Conferences," *Personnel and Guidance Journal,* XLIV, No. 2 (October, 1965), 142-146.

Ninety-five high school seniors and their parents constituted the population of the study. They came from 36 high schools in Wisconsin. No significant differences in any of the areas appeared between the extent of action and the patterns in which parents attended conferences. Where specific and tangible recommendations were made to parents by counselors (especially in the areas of reading and planning, and especially to college-educated parents), extensive action was reported. General discussion seemed not to result in much activity.

147. Johnson, Robert H., M. Delbert Lobb, and Lloyd G. Swanson. "An Extensive Study of Team Teaching and Schedule Modification in Jefferson County, Colorado, School District R-L" *National Association of Secondary School Principals,* XLIV (January, 1960), 79-83.

Seven high schools were involved in the team-teaching approach with a total of approximately 1,500 students participating. It was found that teaching teams produce just as good results in the educational development as teaching working singly with regular classes. Just as good results in pupils' educational development were achieved with a modified schedule as with a regular schedule. No significant differences were found except in English III, which favored team teaching and in English II, which favored the regular teaching.

148. Jones, Emlyn. "Social Studies Requirements in an Age of Science and Mathematics," *Social Education,* XXVII (January, 1963), 17-18.

Sixty-four systems reported that they were requiring world history compared to only 28 ten years earlier. United States history was required by 100 per cent of the school systems involved and there was found to be a decline in the number of systems requiring problems courses. Civics and government were both being moved from ninth and tenth grades to the twelfth grade and the total number of semesters in required social studies was up.

149. Justman, Joseph. "Academic Achievement of Intellectually Gifted Accelerants and Non-accelerants in the Senior High School," *School Review,* LXII (November, 1954), 469-473.

Four New York City schools enrolling large numbers of intellectually gifted students were selected for this study. It was found that when both final marks and Regent's scores were used as criteria, only minor differences were found between groups of accelerants and non-accelerants. The same degree of mastery in the academic areas was shown by accelerants despite the fact that they were a year younger than the non-accelerants.

150. Keating, Raymond F. *"A Study of the Effectiveness of Language Laboratories,"* The Institute of Administrative Research, Teachers College, Columbia University, 1963.

More than 5,000 students in 21 school districts were tested in the study. There were many significant differences favoring the non-lab group, and these differences were primarily at the upper end of the IQ distribution. The high-IQ students were most severely disadvantaged by the inclusion of the lab in the instructional program.

151. Kemp, C. Gratton. "Influence of Dogmatism on the Training of Counselors," *Journal of Counseling Psychology,* IX, No. 2 (1962), 155-157.

Fifty graduate students participated in the study, 25 each in the control and experimental groups. The control group did not engage in a counseling practicum. Without specific training, neither open- nor closed-minded students changed significantly. With training, both high and low D scorers changed significantly toward permissiveness on the Porter Test of Counselor Attitudes. The more closed-minded the student, the greater the change on the Porter Test. The more open-minded the student, the more permissive, and the less the change. The more closed-minded, the greater the discrepancy between the Porter test and actual responses; i.e., less permissive than measured.

152. Klaus, David J. "Programming: A Re-emphasis on the Tutorial Approach," *Audiovisual Instruction,* VI, No. 4. Washington, D.C.: Department of Audiovisual Instruction of the National Education Association, 130-132, 148.

Twenty-five physics classes representing 17 schools participated in the study—a total of roughly 650 students. Auto-instruction did not vastly improve the students' speed of learning or level of attainment.

153. Klauser, Eva L. "A Comparison of a Structural Approach and a Traditional Approach to the Teaching of Grammar in an Illinois Junior High School," *Dissertation Abstracts,* XXVII (1966), 5633.

Subjects for comparison were two groups at each level of the junior high school. At each level, the same teacher taught the two classes being compared. All students made significant gains in achievement. In the ninth and seventh grades, students studying grammar by the structural approach made more significant gains in understanding effective writing than did the groups studying grammar by the traditional approach. There were no significant differences between groups in the eighth grade.

154. Klausmeier, Herbert J. and William Wiersma. "Team Teaching and Achievement," *Education,* LXXXVI (1965-1966), 238-242.

This experiment was carried out in five junior high schools in Racine, Wisconsin, in seventh-grade English and social studies. Team teaching was used for low and average pupils in homogeneous and heterogeneous groupings. Team teaching proved to be slightly better than traditional methods.

155. Knox, Donald Waser. "An Experimental Study of the Effect of a Team-Teaching Program upon Certain Selected Variables (Achievement Anxiety-Social Relations)," *Dissertation Abstracts,* XXVII (August, 1966), 416A-417A.

This study compared team-teaching programs at the Lewis Sands School in Chagrin Falls, Ohio with the self-contained classroom program in existence at the Lewis Sands School. No significant differences were found in arithmetic achievement, language, general anxiety, test anxiety, or in social relations.

156. Koontz, W. F. "Study of Achievement as a Function of Homogeneous Grouping," *Journal of Experimental Education,* XXX (December, 1961), 249-253.

In this study, pupils in five fourth-grade classes were the experimental subjects. Control subjects came from other Norfolk schools. Groups were formed in arithmetic, language, and reading. It was found that homogeneous grouping failed to realize its theoretical possibilities. The control group made higher final-grade equivalents in all subjects and at all levels, but not significantly higher.

157. Kraft, Charles H. "Evaluation of SMSG Grades 7-12," *Dissertation Abstracts,* XXIII (1962), 502.

The problem was to evaluate the mathematics achievements of students using SMSG materials. Ninety-two participating classes in grades seven to twelve were pre-tested and post-tested. Students who were high in both pre-test ability and achievement were equally high in post-test achievement. On standardized achievement tests, SMSG students did as well or better than students do nationwide.

158. Krumboltz, John D. and Barbara Varenhorst. "Molders of Pupil Attitudes," *Personnel and Guidance Journal,* XLIII, No. 5 (January, 1965), 443-446.

Did counselors have any influence in modifying the pupil attitude? Or did parents and peers swing more weight in influencing student opinion? The final sample consisted of 189 ninth-grade pupils in social studies classes in Palo Alto, California. On the average, the greatest agreement was found when statements were attributed to counselors. Agreement was considerably less when statements were attributed to peers and still lower when attributed to parents.

159. Krumboltz, John D. and Wade W. Schroeder. "Promoting Career Planning through Reinforcement" *Personnel and Guidance Journal,* XLIV, No. 1 (September, 1965), 19-25.

Fifty-four eleventh-grade volunteers for educational and vocational counseling were randomly assigned to three treatments. Experimental groups engaged in more external information-seeking behaviors than control groups for females but not males. Model-reinforcement counseling produced significantly more external ISB than control for males but not females. Model-reinforcement counseling was more effective than reinforcement counseling alone for males but not for females. Reinforcement procedures alone were more effective with females than with males.

160. Kumata, Hideya. "Two Studies in Classroom Teaching by Television" in W. Schramm, ed., *The Impact of Educational Television.* Urbana: University of Illinois Press, 1960.

Two sections of a junior-level course in advertising were used. All comparisons were made by simple analysis of variance. There were eight regular assignments during the quarter. For the first seven assignments, no significant F's were produced. In the eighth assignment, a significant difference was found. Face-to-face students got the highest grades, followed by in-studio students and then by TV students. The mid-term examination produced no significant difference. On the final examination, however, the face-to-face students received significantly higher scores.

Experiment II: In view of the significant differences favoring the face-to-face group in the previous experiment, it was decided to rerun the experiment using the same materials and instructor. Analysis of the six regular assignments, the mid-term examination, the final grades, and the four special quizzes produced no significant differences. In the area of attitudes, the second experiment seemed to indicate that the face-to-face teaching situation was the better vehicle for getting attitude change in the desired direction.

Appendix A

161. Kusinitz, Ivan and Clifford Kenney. "Effects of Progressive Weight Training on Health and Physical Fitness of Adolescent Boys," *Research Quarterly,* XXIX (1958), 294-301.

Subjects were tested before and after an eight-week progressive resistance training program. The experimental group participated in the program, but the control group took part only in regularly scheduled physical education classes. Forty-six junior high school boys between 12 and 17 were divided into two groups which were equated on the basis of arm strength, Harvard Step Test scores, age, ponderal index (height-weight relationship), and ethnic origin. In no case did the improvement of the control group significantly exceed the improvement of the experimental group. Medical examinations indicated that no harmful effects were experienced by either the experimental or control group.

162. Lambert, Philip, William L. Goodwin, and William Wiersma. "A Comparison of Pupil Adjustment in Team and Self-Contained Organizations," *Journal of Education Research,* LVIII (March, 1965), 311-314.

The study involved 349 elementary school students in the first year and 381 in the second year. The two different classroom organizations produced only minor differences in adjustment as measured by the California Test of Personality. Only in personal adjustment scores of the first year was there a significant organizational main effect.

163. Lance, Mary Louise. "A Comparison of Gains in Achievement Made by Students of BSCS High School Biology and of Students of a Conventional Course in Biology." Unpublished doctoral dissertation, University of Georgia, 1964.

This study involved 260 ninth- and tenth-graders in and near Athens, Georgia. Pupil traits included age, school, and interactions of course with sex and sex with school. There were no significant relationships to scores made on the final form of the Nelson Biology Test. Scores made by the students on the initial forms of the two tests were found to be significantly related to the scores made on the final forms at the .01 level of confidence.

164. Landis, Carl. "Influence of Physical Education Activities on Motor Ability and Physical Fitness of Male Freshmen," *Research Quarterly,* XXVI (1955), 295-307.

>The study was conducted at the Agricultural and Mechanical College of Texas, with 1,031 incoming freshmen being tested by the Physical Fitness Test. Tumbling-gymnastics and conditioning were significantly superior to the other activities in developing physical fitness. There was no significant difference in weight training, wrestling, volleyball, and boxing in developing physical fitness in students who participated in those activities. All groups were superior to the swimming group.

165. Lawson, Fred Russell. "A Comparative Study of the Achievement of Eighth- and Ninth-Grade Students in Beginning Algebra," *Dissertation Abstracts,* XXII (1961), 1197.

>The data for this study were collected by use of a standardized algebra achievement test administered to 66 eighth-grade students and 62 ninth-grade students in beginning algebra in Muskogee, Oklahoma. Eighth-grade students achieved traditional algebra concepts through study of School Mathematics Study Group materials as well as through study of traditional materials.

166. Lax, John E. "A Comparison of Teaching Methods Used by Superior and Non-Superior Teachers," *Social Studies,* LIII (October, 1962), 171-174.

>Did superior social studies teachers use the same methods in their teaching as the average or below-average teachers? It was found that they used the same methods and activities, but that the extent of use varied greatly in the number of instances. The problems approach was used as the basic approach by a small percentage of superior teachers and an even smaller percentage of non-superior teachers. Teacher-led class discussions stood out as the basic method for presenting social-studies materials in both groups.

167. Leutnegger, Ralph R. and Theodore H. Mueller. "Auditory Factors and the Acquisition of French Language Mastery," *Modern Language Journal,* XLVIII (March, 1964), 141-146.

>All students registered in the beginning course of French at the University of Florida were given the

Appendix A

tests. There was a significant change between performance on the pre-test and post-test. Students performed better in hearing the pitch of French after one year of college French.

168. Lisonbee, Lorenzo K. "The Comparative Effect of BSCS and Traditional Biology upon Student Achievement." Unpublished doctoral dissertation, Arizona State University, 1963.

The purpose of this study was to compare achievement between students of new experimental BSCS High School Biology with students in a traditional or conventional course. Some 252 tenth-grade students were involved. Students in BSCS Biology learned the important core of traditional biology, plus the new, updated biological knowledge incorporated in the BSCS course.

169. Livingston, Howard F. "The Effect of Instruction in General Semantics on the Critical Reading Ability of Tenth-Grade Students," *Dissertation Abstracts,* XXVI (January, 1966), 3783-3784.

Significant differences were found in changes in scores of the experimental group as compared to the change in scores of the control group. No significant difference occurred either between teachers or between teachers and groups. Critical reading ability of tenth-grade students improved as a result of teaching general semantics.

170. Loman, M. LaVerne. "An Experimental Evaluation of Two Curriculum Designs for Teaching First-Year Algebra in a Ninth-Grade Class," *Dissertation Abstracts,* XXII (1961), 502.

Two classes of ninth-grade students enrolled in first-year algebra at Norman, Oklahoma served as subjects for this study. A statistically significant difference in the understanding of basic mathematical concepts in favor of the group using the contemporary program was obtained at the upper one-third intelligence level. No real difference was found between the two groups at either the middle or the lower one-third intelligence level. No difference was found in the achievement of the two groups at any level of intelligence.

171. Lonsdale, Bernard J. and Lorene Marshall. "In-Service Education Programs in Selected California School Districts," *California Journal of Elementary Education,* XXV (August, 1956), 30-51.

> Twenty-two city school districts were visited. Programs included the following practices: (1) planning involving teachers, supervisors, administrators, and consultants; (2) cooperative planning with teacher-education institutions; (3) development of procedures for evaluating the effectiveness of the program; (4) cooperative planning to arrive at long-term goals; and (5) gathering of necessary materials by administrative heads for use by the teachers.

172. Loretan, Joseph O. "Team Teaching: Plus and Minus in New York City's Junior High Schools." *Bulletin of the NASSP,* XLVI, No. 270 (January, 1962), 135-139.

> A group of approximately 120 youngsters reported to the auditoriums for a lesson in basic reading skills. Large-group instruction, balanced with classroom and small-group discussion, seemed to be effective at the junior high school level. Teachers generally felt that large-group situations had a good effect on discipline. They further felt that their students had improved in work habits, attention, interest, and knowledge of the reading skills.

173. Lorge, Sarah W. "Language Laboratory Research Studies in New York City High Schools: Discussion of the Programs and Findings," *Modern Language Journal,* XLVIII (November, 1964), 409-419.

> First-, second-, and third-year high school French classes were studied. Greatest gains were made by the daily lab group using recording-playback equipment. This group made significantly greater gains than all other groups in speech and in listening comprehension. Time spent in lab contributed to conventional learning as well as to listening and speaking skills.

174. Lovell, J. T. "Bay High School Experiment," *Educational Leadership,* XVII (March, 1960), 383.

> The entire second-year class at Bay High School was ranked by ability. Odd-numbered students were grouped by ability and even-numbered students were placed in

a control group heterogeneously. It was found that students in English were the only ones to make greater academic progress when grouped by ability. There was no significant difference in algebra and biology. Ability grouping in the experiment had no significant effect on the acceptance of students by their classmates as measured by the sociogram used. Neither was a significant effect found for the students' acceptance of self and others.

175. Lowe, William T. "Do Social Studies Teachers Want Curriculum Change?" *Social Studies,* LV, No. 3 (March, 1964), 96-99.

How do teachers of one geographic area (Geneva, New York) feel about the need for curriculum study? Two hundred and seven secondary school social studies teachers gave their reactions. The respondents wanted more economics, more geography, more time spent on the emerging regions of the world, etc., but they did not want to give up any time spent on history. These teachers were highly critical of themselves, and were not hesitant to take a position. They wanted greater opportunity to stay abreast of changes in their fields and the time and help necessary for this re-education process.

176. Luckie, William Ronald. "Leader Behavior of Directors of Instruction," *Dissertation Abstracts,* XXV (1964), 1690.

This study attempted to investigate the leader behavior of directors of instruction by use of the Leader Behavior Description Questionnaire. The director of instruction appeared to lead best when he was showing a great deal of consideration to his fellow staff members. Skills in human relations or in maintaining group morale appeared to be of vital concern to the director's satisfactory leader performance.

177. McCallon, Earl L. "Interpersonal Perception Characteristics of Teachers," *Journal of Experimental Education,* XXXIV (Spring, 1966), 97-100.

The sample consisted of 47 fifth- and sixth-grade teachers from an urban school district. (1) Teachers tended to perceive themselves with less favorableness than they perceived the student considered most desirable to teach. (2) Teachers who tended to perceive themselves more favorably tended to perceive the student considered most desirable to teach more favorably. (3) Teachers having taught a greater number of years tended to perceive the student considered least desirable to teach with less favorableness.

178. McFarlan, Robert O. "A Comparative Study of Achievements in Critical Thinking and Factual Knowledge by Rural High School Students of PSSC Physics." Unpublished master's thesis, 1963.

The experiment took place in four different high schools with two classes using the conventional methods (control group) and two classes using the PSSC course (experimental group). PSSC students showed a significant gain in critical thinking over students in the conventional courses; conventional students showed a slight loss in mean critical thinking. In factual knowledge, both groups showed significant gains.

179. McGarvey, Paul. "Programmed Instruction in Ninth-Grade Algebra," *The Mathematics Teacher,* LV, No. 7 (1962), 576-78.
This study involved 19 ninth-grade students enrolled in an algebra improvement class. Programmed material presented a rigid body of material without opportunity for the student to make discoveries for himself.

180. McKinney, Max Terral. "A Study of the Teaching and Use of the New Program Material in Mathematics in Selected Secondary Schools in Alabama," *Dissertation Abstracts,* XXV (1964), 5155.

The study involved 46 secondary school mathematics teachers who were using the new material and 1,007 students. Tests were given to determine if there was a significant difference between the feelings of the teachers and students toward the effectiveness of the new material. In general, the teachers and pupils both had favorable attitudes toward the new materials and programs. Teachers enjoyed teaching the new materials. Students needed elementary training in new mathematics. Some teachers needed preparation in both content and methodology of the new material.

181. McNeil, John. "An Experimental Effort to Improve Instruction through Visual Feedback" *Journal of Educational Research,* LV, No. 6 (March, 1962), 283-285.

   This study attempted to determine whether student teachers who were provided with immediate knowledge of selected effects of their teaching upon pupils during instruction (feedback) would more rapidly acquire a large repertoire of appropriate teaching behaviors. The differences were not significant.

182. McNeil, John D. "Programmed Instruction versus Usual Classroom Procedures in Teaching Boys to Read," *American Educational Research Journal,* I (March, 1964), 113-119.

   A total of 132 children completed the auto-instructional program as kindergartners in two public schools in middle-class communities. Kindergarten boys earned significantly higher scores on the post-test following auto-instruction. After instruction by female teachers, these same boys (who showed superiority to girls after auto-instruction), were inferior to girls on a test covering teacher-taught words. It was concluded that teachers treat boys and girls differently, and that there is an association between teacher behavior and student performance in beginning reading.

183. Mahler, F. L. "A Study of Achievement Differences in Selected Junior High School Gifted Students Heterogeneously or Homogeneously Grouped." Unpublished doctoral dissertation, University of Houston, 1961.

   Experimental and control groups were established at the seventh-grade level in three junior high schools and at the eighth-grade level in one. It was found that students should be homogeneously grouped for reading classes. There was no advantage in homogeneous grouping for arithmetic classes. Grade level was not a factor in achievement gain, and sex was also not a factor.

184. Malan, June R. "An Experiment with a Recently Developed Text for Ninth-Grade Mathematics," United States Office of Education, Bulletin No. 12, 1963, p. 50.

   In this study, the experimental group consisted of four classes, two taught by each of two teachers using the materials of the Development Project in Secondary

Mathematics developed at Southern Illinois University. The control group consisted of two classes taught by another teacher using traditional materials. Students in the experimental group achieved significantly higher.

185. Markland, S. "Scholastic Attainments as Related to Size and Homogeneity of Classes," *Journal of Educational Research,* VI (November, 1963), 63-67.

For this study, a national sample of 150 classes (3,691 pupils), and a South Stockholm sample of 39 classes (1,233 pupils) were used. In the total national sample, 122 comparisons of attainment were made in the three homogeneity groups. Twenty-three favored homogeneous classes, 13 favored heterogeneous classes, and 86 showed no significant differences. It was observed that one factor almost beyond measurement and control is the capability of teachers.

186. Marks, Edmond, et al. "Recommended Curricular Change and Scholastic Performance," *Journal of Counseling Psychology,* XII, No. 1 (1965), 17-22.

A total of 1,526 subjects was drawn from the freshmen class entering the Pennsylvania State University in the fall of 1960. Both students who changed to recommended curricula and those who changed to curricula which were not recommended obtained higher mean grade point averages than those students who did not change. The difference was not significant. With respect to the strength of recommendation, those who had a weaker recommendation obtained a significantly higher mean grade point average. For science curricula, scholastic performance appeared to be more predictable than for non-science curricula.

187. Martin, Gaither Lee and Charles H. R. Over. "Therapy by Television," *AV Communication Review,* IV (1956), 119-130.

The patients for this study were selected from Agnews State Hospital, Agnew, California. They were 141 hospitalized females, classified, with few exceptions, as chronic schizophrenics of various types. Mentally ill patients improved significantly in behavior patterns when given therapy through closed circuit television, especially in the areas of communication, interpersonal relationships, and socialization.

Appendix A

188. Meacham, Ester A. "The Relative Effectiveness of Face-to-Face Lecture versus Instructional Television in a College Clothing Course," *Dissertation Abstracts,* XXIV (July-August, 1963), 276-277.

> Eighty-three students in college classes of home economics were subjects. The results showed no significant difference in the achievement of the two groups as measured by the gain on the objective test, performance test, choice-of-picture test, Graves Design Judgment Test, and by the score on the problem-solving test. There was a significant difference in achievement on laboratory performance favoring the experimental group.

189. Melaragno, Ralph J. "Effect of Negative Reinforcement in Automated Teaching Settings," *Psychological Reports,* VII, (October, 1960), 381-384.

> Twenty-eight paid subjects from freshman mathematics classes of a junior college were assigned to three groups. The lack of significant difference between Group I and Group II indicated that the presence of some negative reinforcement within a teaching sequence did not hinder a student's learning.

190. Meranda, Peter F. and John W. M. Rothney. "Evaluating the Effects of Counseling—Eight Years After," *Journal of Counseling Psychology,* V, No. 3 (1958), 163-168.

> A longitudinal study of the effects of the counseling process was undertaken. Eight hundred and seventy high school sophomores were assigned equally to an experimental group which received intensive counseling for the remaining three years of high school, and to a control group which did not receive counseling on an organized basis. By graduation, 690 subjects remained. With the exception of the unmarried females who did not go on to higher education, the experimental groups were superior to the control groups in all measures.

191. Mikkelson, J. C. "An Experimental Study of Selective Grouping and Acceleration in Junior High School Mathematics." Unpublished doctoral dissertation, University of Minnesota, 1962.

> The subjects grouped for superior ability were 280 students of high mathematics ability selected from

1,600 seventh- and eighth-grade students at Northeast Jr. High in Minneapolis. No differences resulted from grouping junior high students of superior mathematical ability when no adjustments were made in procedures or curriculum. There was some evidence (not conclusive) that removal of the superior mathematics students from the class might have been beneficial to less able students.

192. Mitchell, James V. "Personality Characteristics Associated with Motives for Entering Teaching," *Phi Delta Kappan*, XLV-XLVI (June, 1965), 529-532.

This study involved 85 upper-division female student teachers. It was found that personality characteristics influenced reasons for entering teaching and even choice of teaching level, and there seemed little doubt that the different characteristics associated with the various motives would have a determining influence on the skills, interests, and teaching styles of the prospective teachers. A conscientious attitude towards one's work and the absence of strong tension and anxiety seemed to constitute important and minimal requirements for teaching.

193. Mitchell, Virginia White. "An Analysis of the Grade Expectations and the Actual Achievement of Fourth-, Fifth-, and Sixth-Grade Pupils," *Teachers College Journal*, XXXI (November, 1959), 20-22.

One hundred and seventy-five fourth-, fifth-, and sixth-grade pupils were given intelligence tests from which grade expectancies were determined and achievement tests to determine other grade equivalents. It was found that children who achieved in advance of their actual grade placement still may have been serious underachievers. The wide range of levels of achievement within all of the grade groups rendered non-promotion on the basis of grade placement standards indefensible.

194. Moore, Patricia. "A Language Laboratory Experiment in the Junior High School," *Modern Language Journal*, XLVI (October, 1962), 269-271.

The top three homogeneously grouped seventh-grade French sections were used in this experiment. Fifty per cent of the experimental group showed a marked improvement, while 25 per cent had more errors. On the written test, 50 per cent of the control group showed improvement while 25 per cent increased in the number of errors. On the final examination, five of the six highest papers were written by members of the experimental group.

195. Morris, Ruby Pearl. "A Comparative Analysis of Selected Characteristics of Intellectually Superior Female Students Who Persisted and Those Who Did Not Persist in an Advanced Placement Program," *Dissertation Abstracts,* XXV (1964), 3402.

The twelfth-grade girls from ten senior high schools of a metropolitan public school system were used. No significant differences were obtained between the persisting and non-persisting girls on the dimension of self-sufficiency; persisting girls were characterized by greater social presence and spontaneity. Intellectually superior girls persisted in curricular offering most congruent with self-actualizing processes. Culturally defined "feminine" roles and conflicting societal expectations appeared to concern these girls.

196. Moses, John Irving. "A Comparison of the Results of Achievement with Programmed Learning and Traditional Classroom Techniques in First-Year Algebra at Spring Branch Junior High School, 1961-62," *Dissertation Abstracts,* XXIII, No. 5 (1963), 1559-1560.

The purpose of this study was to determine if any superiority exists in the programmed learning method of instruction as compared to the traditional method of instruction. From the standpoint of total group, there was no appreciable advantage for either method of instruction.

197. Mullin, Daniel W. "An Experimental Study of Retention in Educational TV," *Speech Monographs,* March, 1957.

The subjects were eleventh-grade students of both sexes from three high schools in the same city. Motivation was significantly effective in increasing the retention of both the home viewer and the classroom viewer. Mean scores suggested that the motivated student may learn more at home than in a classroom.

198. Myers, Robert B. "The Development and Implications of a Conception of Leadership for Leadership Education," *Dissertation Abstracts,* XIV (1954), 782.

> The purpose of the study was to develop a conception of leadership. Leadership was a group role, assumed by persons who shared activities, contributed to goals, protected ideals, interpreted reality, and who held values common to the group. The sharing of authority was fundamental to effective leadership education.

199. Nance, Afton D. "Problems of In-Service Education for Teachers," *California Journal of Elementary Education,* XXV (August, 1956), 12-29.

> Data collected from 58 counties and 22 city school districts revealed that all required skill in human relations, ability to analyze situations, and courage to act in the light of knowledge.

200. Nasca, Donald. "Comparative Merits of a Manipulative Approach to Second-Grade Arithmetic," *The Arithmetic Teacher,* XIII (March, 1966), 221-223.

> Second-grade classes in the Campus School at State University College at Brockport, New York were used. The experimental group performed better in computation. The experimental group did significantly better on modern tests and just as well on traditional tests.

201. Neidt, Charles O. and Dalva E. Hedlund. "Student Reactions to High School Language Lab Activities," *Modern Language Journal,* XLIX (December, 1965), 471-475.

> High school classes in French, German, and Spanish at the Fort Collins High School, Colorado were included in the study. The study involved 620 students. Lab tests were ranked as the least effective technique. All classes ranked listening and repeating first, listening and comprehending second, and group conversation third in order of effectiveness.

202. Nelson, Ester. "In-Service Education Programs in California Counties," *California Journal of Elementary Education,* XXV (August, 1956), 12-29.

> Members of the Bureau of Elementary Education visited each county in California to secure first-hand

Appendix A 147

knowledge of in-service education programs for teachers. The following were suggested: (1) development of instruments and procedures for evaluation in terms of changed behavior, (2) improvement of working relationships with college and university instructors to develop courses of maximum value to teachers, and (3) guidance for teachers in selecting courses of greatest value to their professional growth.

203. Nesbitt, William Otto. "An Experimental Study of the Relative Effectiveness on Learning in Selected High School Subjects of the Conventional Methods and a Composite of Procedures Involving Modern Educational Media in Addition to Classes of Varying Sizes, Team Teaching and Teacher Aides," *Dissertation Abstracts,* XXI (December, 1961), 1478.

This study was an analysis of the evidence during the final year of an experiment on staff utilization in Snyder, Texas which lasted three years. There was a significant difference between the two methods of instruction in biology and general science but not in language arts. The difference was in favor of the control classes in biology, and in favor of the experimental classes in general science.

204. Noall, Matthew F. and Lawrell Jensen. "Team Teaching at Roosevelt Junior High School, Duchisne County, Utah," *National Association of Secondary School Principals,* XLIV (January, 1960), 156-163.

The eighth-grade class was scheduled for one two-hour block of time for English, U.S. history and personal citizenship. A team of four teachers was assigned to the project for three periods per day. The eighth-grade students in two other county schools were used as control groups. The combined experimental group achieved higher mean gain scores in the areas of history and total language, but there was no significant difference between the two groups in terms of mean gain scores in reading.

205. Noall, Mathew F. and Gale Rose. "Team Teaching at the Wahlquist Junior High School, Weber County, Utah," *Bulletin of the NASSP,* XLIV, No. 252 (January, 1960), 164-171.

The eighth-grade consisting of 225 pupils was organized into two sections. The subject areas of U.S. history, language arts, and pupil guidance were integrated into a series of resource units. There was no significant difference in the learning outcomes as shown by the standardized tests.

206. Ofman, William and Morton Shaevitz. "The Kinesthetic Method in Remedial Reading," *Journal of Experimental Education,* XXXI (March, 1963), 317-320.

The subjects were 30 full-time students enrolled at the University of California at the Los Angeles Clinic School. The eye-tracing and finger-tracing methods were both more effective than simple reading, but finger-tracing was not more effective than eye-tracing in the acquisition of new material by a random sample of retarded readers.

207. Oldridge, Buff. "Two Roles for Elementary School Guidance Personnel," *Personnel and Guidance Journal,* XLIII, No. 4 (December, 1964), 367-370.

The purpose of the study was to compare experimentally the perceived effectiveness of a guidance staff functioning in a psycho-therapeutic role to that of one with a broader guidance role at the elementary school level. The study was conducted in eastern Los Angeles County with twelve elementary schools, K-6, and five junior high schools, 7-8. The guidance personnel showed no significant preference at the outset but favored the guidance role at the end. Teacher perceptions of pupil change favored no group. Peer perceptions of change favored the control group.

208. Olson, Lowell Ellis. "Teachers', Principals' and Librarians' Perceptions of the School Librarian's Role," *Dissertation Abstracts,* XXVII, Pt. A., 1846.

The sample included 107 secondary schools with full-time librarians in 39 Minneapolis—St. Paul school systems. Responses were received from 246 teachers, 95 principals, and 127 librarians. Teachers, principals, and librarians differed significantly in their perceptions of the school librarian's status, preparation, and functions. Half of the teachers knew that school librarians must take education courses, do student teaching, and become certified as a teacher. All groups agreed that, in existing library programs, technical processing receives most attention; they recommended that administration receive the greatest attention. One-third to

Appendix A

one-half of each group recommended that librarians spend little, if any, time on clerical tasks.

209. Osburn, H. G. and R. S. Melton. "Prediction of Proficiency in a Modern and Traditional Course in Beginning Algebra," *Educational and Psychological Measurement,* XXIII (Summer, 1963), 277-287.

This study was concerned with the Development Project in Secondary Mathematics as Southern Illinois University. The study was conducted at Central High School, Cape Girardeau, Missouri. A battery of aptitude tests was administered to students in an experimental, modern ninth-grade algebra course and to students in a traditional ninth-grade algebra course. For the most part, the aptitude tests were equally valid in predicting proficiency in either course. Spatial and mechanical reasoning tests were more valid for the experimental course than for the traditional course.

210. Paige, Donald Dean. "A Comparison of Team versus Traditional Teaching of Junior High School Mathematics," *Dissertation Abstracts,* XXVII (December, 1966), pp. 1717A-1718A.

This study compared students who were taught mathematics at the seventh- and eighth-grade level by team teaching with students taught by the traditional, single-teacher method. There was no significant difference in the mathematical achievement, in the retention of mathematical achievement, or in the relearning ability of seventh- and eighth-graders whether they were taught by team teaching or by the traditional method.

211. Pella, Milton O. and Chirs Poulos. "A Study of Team Teaching in High School Biology" *Journal of Research in Science Teaching,* I, Issue 5 (1963), 232-240.

Four hundred students were involved in this study. There was no significant difference in achievement, nor was there any significant difference between the boys and girls. Team teaching in Wausau, Wisconsin and traditional teaching procedures were equally effective.

212. Perkins, Hugh. "Classroom Behavior and Underachievement," *American Educational Research Journal,* II, No. 1 (January, 1965), 1-12.

The initial subpopulation consisted of 27 fifth-grade classrooms in upper middle-class communities of a county school system in Maryland. Student work-oriented behavior and roles that facilitated learning were associated with increased academic achievement, whereas criticism by the teacher and withdrawal by the student were associated with decreased academic achievement.

213. Popham, W. James. "Tape-Recorded Lectures in the College Classroom." *AV Communication Review,* IX (March-April, 1961), pp. 109-118.

Subjects for this experiment were 55 students enrolled in an educational research course. Twenty-seven students were in the experimental group, which was taught by means of tape-recorded lectures, and 27 students were in a conventional lecture-discussion situation. There were no significant differences in the achievement of either group on any of the three measures used.

214. Rabkin, Lezlie Y. "The Dogmatism of Teachers," *Journal of Teacher Education,* XVII (Spring, 1966), 47-50.

The purpose of this study was to learn, within the range of the sample, whether teachers were excessively dogmatic. The Rokeach Dogmatism Scale was administered to 107 school teachers. Correlations between dogmatism and age, sex, years of experience, religious affiliations, grades taught, and marital status were all nonsignificant. The veteran teachers (more than ten years experience) did not score significantly higher on the Dogmatism Scale. Excessive dogmatism or closed-mindedness was not a general characteristic of this group of educators.

215. Rice, Jimmy Marshall. "A Study of Attitudes of Elementary Teachers toward Modern Mathematics Programs," *Dissertation Abstracts,* XXVI (1964), 1433.

A 45-item Likert-type attitude scale was administered to elementary teachers of school systems within a 120-mile radius of Oklahoma State University. A total of 608 responses was received and 400 were treated statistically by use of the analysis of variance. Attitudes toward modern mathematics programs were not independent of the total amount of training in all areas.

Appendix A

The attitudes of those teachers with more than four years college work were more favorable than the attitudes of teachers with four years or less. Attitudes toward modern mathematics programs were independent of age, experience, and sex.

216. Richardson, Richard E. and Clyde E. Blocker. "An Item Factorization of the Faculty Attitude Survey," *Journal of Experimental Education,* XXXIV (Spring, 1966), 89-93.

Six public community colleges of varying sizes and types of control, with a total of 231 staff members, were involved in this study. There were different, reasonably unique categories or dimensions of faculty morale. These seemed to be based on (1) supervision, (2) self-integration, (3) institutional environment, and (4) employment records. College faculty morale was a composite of many individual factors.

217. Richman, Paul Tobias. "The Effect of Prestige Suggestion on Science Teachers' Acceptance of New Curriculum," *Dissertation Abstracts,* XXV (1965), 328.

The subjects were teachers with at least five years of teaching experience from twenty-three states and from the Canadian provinces of Alberta, Manitoba, British Columbia, and Saskatchewan. Science teachers, when exposed to a physical science course outline allegedly written over a period of three years, accepted the outline at a significantly higher level than did science teachers who received the identical communication allegedly written over a shorter period of time (five days). A significantly higher mean acceptance was reported from science teachers receiving a physical science course outline from a group of research scientists (high social status) than was reported from science teachers receiving the same outline from a group of laboratory technicians (low social status).

218. Rollins, Sidney P. "Ungraded High Schools: Why Those Who Like Them Love Them," *The Nation's Schools,* LXXIII, No. 4 (April, 1964), 110, 130.

This study was based on reports from Satellite High School, Nova High School, and Melbourne High School, all of Florida, and from Middletown High School of Rhode Island. Pupil progress ranged from a year or more ahead of where pupils would have been had they attended a graded secondary school to a half-year behind the usual achievement at a given grade level. The dropout rate was drastically lower than the national rate. Pupils were grouped not along artifical grade standards, but rather in terms of their own needs and abilities. Teachers who had no experience with ungraded organization frequently found that adjusting to it was difficult. Several lesson plans were required for the same class.

219. Rosenbloom, Paul C. "Minnesota National Laboratory Evaluation of SMSG, Grades 7-12," *Reports on Student's Achievement in SMSG Courses,* Newsletter No. 10. Stanford, California: School Mathematics Study Group, Stanford University, 1961, p. 12-26.

This study was undertaken to determine if teacher characteristics affect student achievement in SMSG courses. A crude measure of teacher qualifications was set up in terms of experience, grades in undergraduate and graduate courses in mathematics, activities in professional organizations, and contributions to the achievement of mathematics teaching. It was found that there were few significant correlations between student achievement and the factors of teacher qualifications which were measured.

220. Rottmann, Leon H. "The Effectiveness of High School Television-Correspondence Instruction," *Dissertation Abstracts,* XXI (November-December, 1960), 1464.

This study was designed to evaluate the extent to which the television-correspondence study method of instruction affected the acquisition of knowledge and the development of attitudes at different levels of school ability. In the achievement evaluation, there were no significant differences between the treatment groups. In the Method subtest in all subjects, the differences between groups yielded results which were statistically significant favoring the control group. Although in some areas, students in TV-correspondence instruction achieved as well as those taught by conventional methods, their attitudes were less favorable.

221. Roughead, William George. "An Experiment in Tenth-Grade Modern Mathematics," United States Office of Education, Bulletin No. 8, 1960, p. 42.

A unit including an introduction to set theory, Venn diagrams, and the graphing of inequalities and equations was developed and taught for six weeks to an unselected average tenth-grade class. It was found that (1) certain college-level materials on modern mathematics could be successfully taught to average tenth-grade students, (2) greater understanding of basic mathematical concepts could be achieved through the modern topics than through the traditional topics, and (3) the achievement of the class was average as far as the traditional topics were concerned.

222. Ruddell, Arden K. "The Results of a Modern Mathematics Program," *The Arithmetic Teacher,* IX (October, 1962), 330-335.

Four seventh-grade classes from an intermediate school in a southern California community constituted the sample for this study. In no instance did the control group score significantly higher than the experimental group, whereas the experimental group scored significantly higher on five of the sixteen basic analyses. In every test of an hypothesis, the higher-intelligence group scored significantly higher than the low-intelligence group. Significant differences in favor of the high achievers on the arithmetic pretests were obtained in most instances. It was found that children taught a program of modern mathematics score as high or higher than children taught a program of traditional mathematics under comparable conditions.

223. Russell, David R. "Intra-Class Grouping for Reading Instruction in the Intermediate Grades," *Journal of Education Research,* XXXIX (February, 1946), 462-470.

Pupils who "circle" for reading were selected in three schools rated as below average, average, and above average in socio-economic status for the city. Intrinsic factors in the instructional program such as material used, teacher's knowledge of the individual child, and efficient and democratic classroom procedures were more important than any external arrangement for reading instruction.

224. Sandefur, Joseph T. "A Study of the Scholastic and Social Implications of Remedial Reading Classes in Selected Senior High Schools, *Dissertation Abstracts,* XIX (1959), 1977-8.

Three hundred retarded readers were selected to participate in the study. The remedial students tended to make higher achievements in reading than did the control group. Comprehension was more significantly improved by remedial training in reading than was vocabulary. Remedial training in reading did not decrease personal and social maladjustments.

225. Sawyer, Robert Lee. "An Investigation of the Effectiveness of the Program Recommended by the Physical Science Study Committee," *Dissertation Abstracts,* XXIV, No. 12, Part I (1964), 5254-5255.

This study attempted to measure the effectiveness of the proposed PSSC program compared to the traditional physics program. In an exam that attempted to combine the objectives of the two programs as equally as possible, the tendency was for the non-PSSC students to score higher than the PSSC students.

226. Sax, Gilbert and John R. Ottina. "The Arithmetic Achievement of Pupils Differing in School Experience," *California Journal of Educational Research,* IX (January, 1958), 15-19.

This experimental investigation was undertaken to study the effects of dissimilar curricula on arithmetic computation and understanding. Significant differences were found between the two groups on a special non-computational test of arithmetic meanings at the seventh and eighth grades only. It was also found that third- and fourth-grade pupils from "conventional" schools made a significantly higher score on a standardized computation test of arithmetic than did the corresponding "progressive" group. This difference was reduced to chance at the fifth, sixth, and seventh grades.

227. Schiffman, Gilbert B. "An Investigation of the Effectiveness of Two Pedagogical Procedures in the Remediation of Remedial Retarded Readers," *Dissertation Abstracts,* XXVI (1965), 1434.

The study was undertaken to determine the relative effectiveness of three types of reading programs in the remediation of reading difficulties. The difference in gain for the remedial and corrective groups was not statistically significant, but the difference in gain for the remedial and developmental groups was statistically

Appendix A 155

significant. Secondary pupils in the corrective group scored higher than pupils in the developmental group, and this difference was statistically significant.

228. Schiller, Mary Philomene. "The Effects of the Functional Use of Certain Skills in Seventh-Grade Social Studies," *Journal of Educational Research,* LVII (December, 1963), 201-204.

Tests were given to 288 seventh-grade pupils attending ten parochial schools in St. Louis, Missouri. It was found that, in the analysis of final history scores, no statistical difference existed between the final history means of the experimental group and the control group when the scores were classified according to the method used.

229. Schmieding, Orville A. "An Investigation of Efficacy of Counseling and Guidance Procedures with Failing Junior High School Students," *School Counselor,* XIV, No. 2 (November, 1966), 74-79.

Students who had failed at least one academic subject were chosen from the seventh and eighth grades of four junior high schools. Groups that were provided counseling and guidance procedures rated statistically higher on three of the five variables.

230. Schuff, Robert V. "A Comparative Study of Achievement in Mathematics at the Seventh- and Eighth-Grade Levels under Two Approaches, School Mathematics Study Group and Traditional," *Dissertation Abstracts,* XXIII (1962), 558-559.

The measurements used to determine effectiveness were achievement scores on STEP and COOP mathematics tests. Subjects were 172 eighth-grade and 216 seventh-grade students in the junior high school of Roseville, Minnesota. If the tests used in measuring the outcomes were valid, the traditional materials proved to be more effective.

231. Schuster, Edgar H. "How Good is the New Grammar?" *English Journal,* L (September, 1961), 392-397.

This study attempted to determine how much grammar students could learn through a wholly structural approach. Four classes in Cheltenham High School,

Wyncote, Pennsylvania made up the sample. The type of grammar studied affected neither the ability to punctuate nor the knowledge of function units. New grammar was superior to the traditional for teaching parts of speech. The change in writing ability was relatively small for all classes.

232. Seeman, Melvin. "A Note on Leader Effectiveness" in *Social Status and Leadership: The Case of the School Executive.* Columbus, Ohio: Bureau of Educational Research, 1960, pp. 84-92.

Seventy-seven leaders (superintendents and principals) and a sample of teachers in each of 26 Ohio systems made up the subjects. Teachers favored high communication and change, low separatism, and low domination. Teachers who rated the leader high in community status and who saw great difference in status between themselves and the leader generally evaluated him highly as an organizational leader. Leaders who rated themselves high in status and who saw great status difference between themselves and their teachers were evaluated highly by their subordinates. Leaders who underrated the teachers' status were accorded low evaluation by their subordinates.

233. Seibert, Warren F. and Jurgen M. Honig. "A Brief Study of Televised Laboratory Instruction," *AV Communication Review,* VIII (May-June, 1960), 115-123.

Subjects were 70 volunteers obtained through a psychology department. Although the instruction produced measureable effects, it apparently made no difference whether groups were taught by conventional means or by means of television.

234. Sharkan, William W. "An Evaluation of the Team Organization Plan of Staff Utilization in Relationship to the Educational Development of Students in the Junior High Schools of Allentown, Pennsylvania," *Dissertation Abstracts,* XXIII (April, 1963), 3742.

Eighty students were selected from each of the four junior high schools in Allentown by a random sampling technique. There were some significant differences favoring the development of the groups taught under "team organization." Twenty-six out of the 40 comparisons in the development of high-ability groups favored the "team-organization" plan. Both low- and high-ability students improved in their educational development in the knowledge and skills when taught by the "team-organization" plan.

235. Silagyi, Dezo V. "A Critical Analysis of Attitudes of Selected Elementary Students toward Television Teaching in the Detroit Television Teaching Project," *Dissertation Abstracts,* XXII (July-September, 1961), 128.

The experimental population consisted of 2,840 pupils enrolled in larger-than-normal classes in eight schools in Detroit, Michigan. Students had to listen more carefully to an on-camera teacher than to a classroom teacher. Opinions of the pupils in the area of personal relationships were positive. With regard to personal achievement, the pupils reflected that they were learning as much by television as they would if they were taking the identical subject in a regular class.

236. Slaichert, William M. and Marion L. Stephens, Jr. "The Effectivenss of a Programmed Text in Plane Geometry," *Journal of Educational Measurement,* LVII (July-August, 1964), 542-544.

The Temac Plane Geometry Course was selected as the programmed material in the Littleton, Colorado, public schools. Teacher-made and standardized tests were used. Where differences existed, the control group scored higher than the experimental group. The fact that no significant differences were found on the final test indicated that control and experimental groups were equal at the end of the experiment.

237. Smith, Frederick R. "The Academic Achievement of Academically Talented Students," *Journal of Educational Research,* LVI, No. 5 (January, 1963), 255-259.

Four schools in Michigan, having special programs for the academically talented, were selected for the evaluative phase of the study. Academic achievements of the talented students were not significantly greater than those of similar students enrolled in regular college-preparatory courses in the same subjects.

238. Somit, Albert, "Evaluating the Effects of Social-Science Instruction," *Journal of Higher Education,* XXVI (June, 1955), 319-322.

> This study attempted to determine the relationship between the classroom study of political problems and inclination to engage in political activities. Subjects were undergraduate liberal arts college students enrolled in two social-science courses. On all scales used, average scores changed less than two points despite exposure to the courses.

239. Spencer, R. C. "Comparisons of Televised with Teaching Machine and Instructor Presentation of English Grammar" in *Comparative Research on Methods and Media for Presenting Programmed Courses in Mathematics and English,* pp. 57-63. Cooperative Project under the direction of C. R. Carpenter and L. P. Greenhill, The Pennsylvania State University, University Park, Pennsylvania, 1962.

> Two simultaneous experiments were conducted, one involving 27 college freshmen and the other 43 high school students. Both groups showed significant learning gains, but there were no significant differences between the groups. In the college groups, no significant differences of achievement were found between the groups. Those students receiving face-to-face instruction had more favorable attitudes toward their method of instruction than did the television group.

240. Spencer, Richard E. and Edmond L. Seguin. "The Relative Effects of Earphone and Loudspeakers as a Means of Presenting a Listening Test in a Foreign Language," *Modern Language Journal,* XLVIII (October, 1964), 346-349.

> The subjects for this experiment were 66 undergraduate students in German III. The performance of the listening test for the earphone group was somewhat superior to performance on the same test by the loudspeaker group. There were no significant effects on performance in reading which resulted from group differences.

241. Stevens, Deon Orlo. "Analysis of Change: A Comparative Study of Mathematics Texts Published for Elementary School Children for the Eight-Year Period, 1956-1964," *Dissertation Abstracts,* XXVI, 5140.

> Studies were made of seven leading text-book series to determine the degree of change in the traditional

language of elementary school mathematics, the traditional material that had been introduced into contemporary arithmetic, and the degree of change in grade placement of elementary school arithmetic topics. There had been an increase of more than 40 per cent in the total vocabulary load in elementary mathematics. Relatively little of the traditional criterion terminology had been dropped from the entire elementary arithmetic vocabulary. The majority of eliminated topics appeared in contemporary material at different grade levels.

242. Stewart, John W. "Influence of Public School Music Education as Revealed by a Comparison of Forty Selected High School Music and Non-Music Students," *Dissertation Abstracts,* XXII (February, 1962), 2882-2883.

Subjects of the study were students at one urban high school. Statistically significant differences between music and non-music students were found. School music had a primary influence on development of performance, related skill, ability, knowledge, nurture of musical interest, and the attitude of all students regarding the appropriateness and purpose of school music. Music education was the primary outlet for music interests in the high school and had a secondary influence on post-high school music making among its participants and on the creation of musical interests. Home musical environment was the primary influence on development of interest in music.

243. Stickell, David W. "A Critical Review of the Methodology and Results of Research Comparing Televised and Face-to Face Instruction," *Dissertation Abstracts,* XXIV (January-February, 1964), 3239-3240.

On the basis of experimental comparisons judged interpretable, which mode of instruction is more effective as measured by achievement tests—the televised or the face-to-face mode? All ten of the interpretable comparisons and twenty of the partially interpretable comparisons yielded no significant difference. Two hundred and fifty comparisons were studied.

244. Storlie, Theodore R. "Selected Characteristics of Teachers Whose Verbal Behavior Is Influenced by an In-Service Course in Interaction Analysis." Unpublished doctoral dissertation, University of Minnesota, 1961.

This study dealt with relationships between selected characteristics of teachers and changes in verbal behavior. The in-service course produced a significant increase in the use of indirect influence in 37 of the 51 teachers in this sample; but the hypothesis regarding relationships between personality characteristics and change in indirect influence was not supported.

245. Sweet, Raymond and Peter Dunn-Rankin. "An Experiment in Team Teaching Seventh-Grade Arithmetic," *School Science and Mathematics,* LXVII, No. 5, 341-344.

The 1,100 students at Brookside Junior High were homogeneously grouped in all classes. The experiment was conducted using two of the top sections that were originally scheduled for mathematics during the same period but under two different instructors. Although no objective evaluation in comparison to a control group of equal ability was made, the general opinion of both the instructors and their visitors was that it seemed to be at least equal to the traditional self-contained classroom.

246. Sutman, Frank X. and Michael Yost. "A Modified Team Approach in Seventh-Grade Science," *Journal of Research in Science Teaching,* III (1965), 275-279.

This study involved 256 pupils. In teaching retention and understanding of energy-machines and magnetism-electricity to above-average, seventh-grade students, a modified team approach utilizing the capabilities of a master teacher was most effective.

247. Taffel, Alexander. "An Evaluation of a Team Method of Teaching High School Physics to Academically Talented Students," *Dissertation Abstracts,* XXII (1962), 4297.

Fifty-five pairs of students at the Bronx High School of Science were matched for age, sex, grade, science and mathematics scores, intelligence quotient, and pretest scores on the Dunning Physics Test. The study revealed no significant or educationally important differences in either achievement or variabilities between the experimental and control groups. The overall attitude of students of the team was favorable.

248. Tallent, John B. "An Experimental Evaluation of the

Appendix A

Teaching of English Grammar by Traditional and Structural Methods," *Dissertation Abstracts,* XXII (1962), 2392.

Two parallel groups of tenth-grade students in the same institution were taught grammar by different methods for a year: mechanics of expression, effectiveness of expression, and reading comprehension. There were no significant differences between the groups.

249. Taylor, Bob L. "Factors Influencing In-Service Teacher Education Programs," *Journal of Educational Research,* LII (May, 1959), 336-338.

A random sample of 100 high schools in Indiana was used. The study attempted to determine the status of in-service education in the public senior high schools in Indiana via five variables: (1) size of enrollment, (2) number of teachers, (3) total assessed valuation in the district, (4) assessed valuation per pupil, and (5) size of the community in which the school was located. Statistical analysis revealed a positive correlation which was statistically significant for all factors except the fourth (assessed valuation per pupil).

250. Thelen, H. A. "Grouping for Teachability," *Theory Into Practice,* II (April, 1963), 81-89.

Fifteen teachers were selected who were located in eight junior high and elementary schools in Illinois, Wisconsin, and Indiana. All students were eighth grade or above. Compatible classes were found to be more manageable and they resulted in higher teacher goal attainment. The compatible class facilitated the execution of the teacher's purposes, but compatibility grouping did not make him a different or better educator. Teachers of compatible classes were more satisfied and gave higher grades.

251. Thomson, Scott D. "An Analysis of Achievement Outcomes: Team Teaching and Traditional Classes," *Dissertation Abstracts,* XXIV (February, 1964), 3240.

Two hundred and nine senior students in Sunnyvale, California were subjects for the study. In measuring achievement immediately upon completion of the unit, the control group achieved significantly better. In measuring learnings twenty days after termination of the unit, the experimental group did significantly better. In the surprise test, no significant differences resulted.

252. Tower, Melvin M. "A Study of Orientation and In-Service Education Practices in the Indianapolis Public Schools," *Educational Administration and Supervision,* XLII (April, 1956), 219-229.

> This study attempted to determine to what degree the orientation and in-service education practices were meeting the needs of beginning experienced and inexperienced teachers. Beginning experienced teachers gained more help from orientation and in-service practices than did beginning inexperienced teachers. All groups agreed that the most helpful activities included individual conferences and small-group meetings on common instructional problems.

253. Traweek, Melvin W. "The Relationship Between Certain Personality Variables and Achievement through Programmed Instruction," *California Journal of Educational Research,* XV (November, 1964), 215-220.

> The population used in this study was 186 white students from six fourth-grade classes enrolled in the city schools of Tuscaloosa, Alabama. There was no significant difference between the mean intelligence quotient of the successful and unsuccessful learners. It was hypothesized that, in this instructional atmosphere, the less intelligent may be able to achieve beyond their expected performance as a result of the classroom setting and the nature of the learning theory involved.

254. Trotter, Charles Earl. "A Fortran Computer Program Designed to Identify the Physical Facilities for a Public Secondary School Instructional Materials Center," *Dissertation Abstracts,* XXV (1964), 2888.

> Primary sources of data were literature, publications by industry, authorities in the field of educational administration, and interviews with recognized authorities. There was a growing awareness of values of an instructional materials center designed for individualized learning. No optimum design has yet been put to practical use.

255. Troutner, Howard LaVerne. "An Investigation into the Apparent Effects of Retainment on the Growth and Behavioral Trait-Characteristic Patterns of Elementary School

Appendix A

Children in Three Socio-Economic Areas." Unpublished master's thesis, The Ohio State University, Columbus, Ohio, 1961.

>Five teachers were contacted and 53 children were used in this investigation. A broad spectrum of differences occurred between cases in the degree of improvement or lack of improvement. Children who were promoted "on trial" tended to make a more satisfactory adjustment than did those youngsters who were retained. A substantial loss of desirable trait-characteristics was experienced when a child was placed. Not one case of grade placement in this study showed improvement during the year of abnormal promotion.

256. Trowbridge, Leslie Walter. "A Comparison of the Objectives of Traditional High School Physics with the Objectives of the Physical Science Study Committee Course, and an Analysis of the Instructional Materials of the PSSC Course," *Dissertation Abstracts,* XXII (1961), 812.

>One hundred PSSC teachers and 100 traditional high school teachers in 19 North Central Association states were asked to respond to a questionnaire. PSSC teachers and traditional teachers differed significantly in the responses to the 72 objectives of high school teaching. The degree of agreement was strongly affected by the factors of school involvement, years of teaching experience, and class size.

257. Truax, Robert Lloyd. "A Study of Factors Which Influence Curriculum Change in Secondary School Mathematics," *Dissertation Abstracts,* XXVI (1964), 1438.

>An intensive survey was conducted of secondary schools in south Arkansas. The enrollment of a school did not influence the content of the mathematics courses. However, small schools tended to have a more limited number of mathematics courses offered in their curriculum. Membership in professional organizations, professional reading, and workshop attendance were all significantly higher in the schools where modern mathematics programs were taught.

258. Ulrich, John H. "An Experimental Study of the Acquisition of Information from Three Types of Recorded Television Presentations," *Speech Monographs* (March, 1957).

This study attempted to determine whether eighth-grade pupils retained more information by observing a kinescope recording of a straight lecture when using no visual aid, the same lecture using visual aids handled by the lecturer, or the same lecture with visual aids flashed on the screen. Whether the visual aids were handled by the lecturer or appeared on the screen seemed to have little effect on the recall of the information. Differences between lecturers employing visual aids and those not employing visual aids tended to disappear after thirty days.

259. Vance, Kenneth. "Professional Status of School Librarians in Michigan Public Secondary Schools Enrolling 500 or More Students," *Dissertation Abstracts,* XXIII (1963), 3391.

Questionnaires were sent to 225 school librarians in 224 accredited schools. Respondents generally met North Central and AASL criteria in regard to academic and professional training and certification. Schools did not entirely meet the specifications in terms of number of personnel. Librarians held the status of teachers and nearly all respondents expressed considerable satisfaction with school librarianship as a profession.

260. Walker, Jerry L. "What Do Student-Teachers Know About Libraries?" *School Libraries,* XVI (Winter, 1967), 17-23.

A 13-item questionnaire to test teachers' knowledge of the availability and use of library resources and services was given to 85 student teachers. Student teachers had very limited knowledge of the library resources available to them. Student teachers had very limited concepts of how the library and the librarian could have been of service to them in their teaching. Most viewed library services as adjuncts to their teaching, not as important, integral parts of it.

261. Walters, Louis. "Ninth-vs-Tenth Grade Biology—A Comparison of Achievement," *Journal of Research in Science Teaching,* I (1963), 170-176.

The subjects for this study were students in University High School, the laboratory high school of the College of Education of the University of Minnesota. The experiment required a minimum of two years for completion. When selected standardized measures were

Appendix A

used, no differences in the achievement of total classes of ninth- and tenth-graders appeared. When a full range of abilities was represented in a class, biology could have been taught in the ninth grade as effectively as in the tenth grade. When tested on selected areas of biology, there appeared to be no significant differences in the achievement of ninth- and tenth-graders.

262. Warnken, Robert G. and Thomas F. Siess. "The Use of the Cumulative Record in the Prediction of Behavior," *Personnel and Guidance Journal,* XLIV, No. 3 (November, 1965), 231-237.

A group of 116 male schizophrenic veterans, all born between 1917 and 1934, were selected from a VA mental hospital. A control sample of equal size, matched for year of birth and sex, was randomly selected from the Minneapolis school cumulative records. In senior high school, 69.4 per cent of the schizophrenic subjects had no record of extra-curricular activities and were described at least once by one of the differentiating terms from the teacher's personality descriptions.

263. West, Jesse W. "A Study of Grouping." Unpublished master's thesis, The Ohio State University, 1961.

Selected test data of matched groups of ten students in the high-, average-, and low-achievement levels at Galion High School were collected and analyzed. The results of grouped and non-grouped students were compared. Personal interviews with the teachers were conducted to obtain their reactions to working with grouped students. It was found that the homogeneous grouping procedures showed overall improvement among all ability groups except high achievers. Low and average achievers made greater academic improvement when homogeneously grouped. Teachers felt that there was marked improvement in interest, discipline, work habits and faculty relationships due to grouping.

264. West, LeRoy C. "Effectiveness of a Television-Correspondence-Study Method of In-Service Education." Unpublished doctoral dissertation, University of Florida, 1961.

Two hundred and sixty-two teachers in three viewing areas were enrolled in the course. The data gathered sustained and supported the fact that the televised-correspondence-study method is validated as a method of in-service education of teachers.

265. Westley, Bruce H. and Harvey K. Jacobson. "Dimensions of Teachers' Attitudes toward Instructional Television," *AV Communication Review,* X (May-June, 1962), 179-185.

Madison Public Schools in Wisconsin carried out a study of two experimental mathematics courses produced by the Wisconsin School of the Air. The teachers' attitudes were highly favorable to instructional television. They consistently rejected the idea that the television teacher represented a threat to the classroom teacher.

266. White, Robert H. "The Effect of Structural Linguistics on Improving English Composition Compared to that of Prescriptive Grammar in the Absence of Grammar Instruction," *Dissertation Abstracts,* XXVII (1967), 5032-5033.

The study included three average seventh-grade classes located in a mixed socio-economic neighborhood. The structural linguistics group showed greater improvement in writing ability on tests of writing skill. The teaching of structural linguistics had a significantly greater effect than traditional grammar or the absence of grammar on improved composition.

267. White, Robert William. "The Relative Effectiveness of a Team Teaching Method in High School Biology Instruction," *Dissertation Abstracts,* XXIII (May, 1963), 4271-4272.

This study attempted to determine if any significant differences existed between biology classes taught by individual teachers and by team teaching. There were no significant differences in achievement when comparing the trend lines of means for the experimental and control groups.

268. Wiley, Frank A. "A Study of Teacher Relationships Considered to be Associated With Readiness and Non-Readiness for Curriculum Change," *Dissertation Abstracts,* XXVI (1965), 5312.

Six hundred teachers participated by responding with a scale to provide a measure of readiness for curriculum change and to ascertain teacher judgments toward certain working relationships. There was a significant difference between teachers ready and non-ready for curriculum change in schools active in curriculum change as to: teacher-teacher relations, teacher-administrator relations, teacher-parent relations, and teacher-pupil relations. There was also a significant difference with regard to teacher-parent relations and teacher-pupil relations. Secondary teachers with fewer than ten years experience and with attendance at five or more summer sessions were more ready for change.

269. Williams, Emmet D. and Robert W. Shuff. "Comparative Study of SMSG and Traditional Mathematics Text Material," *The Mathematics Teacher,* LVI (November, 1963), 495-504.

The Roseville School System was designated by the Minnesota National Laboratory as an experimental center for the trial use of the SMSG text units for Grades seven, eight, and nine. In general, for Grade seven, the SMSG group made greater gains at the lower-ability levels, while the traditional groups made slightly greater gains at both middle- and upper-ability levels. At the eighth-grade level, the mean gain for the traditional group was greater on both measuring instruments. Students whose eighth-grade mathematics background involved work with SMSG materials neither measured nor gained significantly more in achievement in mathematics. None of the differences between means proved significant.

270. Wittich, W. A., Milton O. Pella, and C. A. Wedemeyer. "The Wisconsin Physics Film Evaluation Project," *AV Communication Review,* VIII (May-June, 1960), 156-157.

In this study, 162 30-minute film lessons on high school physics were used. A test which included text and film items showed no significant differences between experimental and control groups. The experimental group was superior in learning film-only items. The Ohio test scores were no different. The control group retained more after three months.

271. Wolfe, Frank A. "An Experimental Study of a System in English Grammar," *Dissertation Abstracts,* XXVII (1966), 4138.

Six classes in seventh-grade English in a public junior-senior high school were used. There were significant gains in vocabulary, reading comprehension, capitalization, and punctuation as well as reading graphs and tables, but there was no significant difference between the experimental and control groups.

272. Wright, Robert Earl. "A Comparison of Student Achievement in Modern Mathematics and Traditional Mathematics in Relation to Ability Grouping," *Dissertation Abstracts,* XXVI (1965), 3178.

This study attempted to compare achievement gains among eighth-grade students when instruction was presented from three different mathematical approaches (two programs of modern mathematics and one of traditional mathematics). Based on test scores resulting from the modern mathematics test, there were significant differences favoring the modern mathematics program. When traditional tests were used, no significant differences were apparent.

273. Yourd, John L. "Locally Operated In-Service Programs of Selected High Schools in Five Midwestern States," *Dissertation Abstracts,* XXIV (1964), 4592.

Data were gathered in a series of interviews in 60 high schools. Teachers had some opportunity to participate in planning in-service activities, but little in evaluating them. Laymen were involved in educational planning primarily when a public vote on school matters was pending. Size of school district was related to the value of in-service activities.

274. Zahn, Richard D. "The Effect upon Student Teachers' Attitudes of Training in Interaction Analysis and the Attitudes of Cooperating Teachers." A paper presented as part of a symposium on interaction analysis held in conjunction with the American Educational Research Association Convention, February, 1965, in Chicago.

This study involved 92 students majoring in elementary education undergoing their initial student-teaching experience during their junior year at Glassboro State College, New Jersey. Instruction and supervision of student teachers using interaction analysis appeared to be related to a positive change in the teaching attitude of the student. The student teacher's attitude

Appendix A

was affected more by the cooperating teacher using conventional techniques than by college supervisors using interaction analysis.

275. Ziebarth, Raymond Allan. "The Effect of Experimental Curricula on Mathematics Achievement in High School," *Dissertation Abstracts,* XXIV (1964), 4593.

This study investigated the relative effectiveness of curricular materials developed by SMSG on the mathematics achievement of the University of Minnesota high school students. Significant differences at the one-per cent level were found between initial and final mean achievement scores for each of the groups. No significant differences between initial and final variances were found for the SMSG groups while some were found for the control groups. No significant differences in mean achievement were found between the SMSG and control groups at the ninth- and tenth-grade levels after initial differences between the groups were held constant.

276. Zimmerman, Helen. "Physical Performance of Children Taught by Special Teachers and by Classroom Teachers," *Research Quarterly,* XXX (1959), 356-362.

This study was conducted to compare the physical performance scores of elementary school children taught by special physical education teachers with those children in a similar school where physical education was taught by the regular classroom teachers. Boys and girls of grades five through eight were included in the study. Boys taught by special teachers exceeded the performance of comparable boys taught by classroom teachers, and the difference was statistically significant. Girls taught by special teachers exceeded the performances of comparable girls. The differences were statistically significant for 14 of the comparisons.

277. Zweibelon, I. M. Bahmuller and L. Lyman. "Team Teaching and Flexible Grouping in the Junior High School Social Studies," *Journal of Experimental Education,* XXIV, No. 1 (Fall, 1965), 20-24.

The demonstration group consisted of approximately 100 pupils at each grade level (7-8-9), with one class from each of four ability groups in each grade. The control-group samples were selected student by student to match the individuals in the demonstration samples. Significant changes in attitude were found between the team-taught samples versus the control groups. Through a list of 80 statements reflecting attitudes toward school, social studies, peers, democracy, and newspapers, it was shown that the team-taught samples had better attitudes in May than in September.

Appendix B

A Plan for Organizing a College Within a University

On the pages which follow is described a sample set of by-laws for organizing a college of education within a university which would be capable of systematic and rational change. In effect, these by-laws set forth a basis for decision-making within a university setting which presumes accountability different from the traditional "line of authority" plan. Authority has been deliberately distributed according to function, and such a plan, were it to be implemented, would necessitate a different conception of personal and professional responsibility for all persons involved in university work: professors, administrators, and students.

These by-laws should be viewed as one way of effecting the rationale described in this book. Other organizational arrangements could be developed, too, and the reader is encouraged to generate propositions of his own which would conceptualize new and different approaches to the governance of university communities.

By-laws Regarding the Purposes, Organization, and Functions of the College of Education at _____ University.

These by-laws describe the purposes, organization, and functions of the College of Education at_____University. The basic intent of these by-laws is to provide for a government of and by the faculty of the College which will enable that group to organize itself so that the clarification of purpose through policy; the implementation of purpose through teaching, research, service, and administration; and the evaluation of policy and its implementation can occur in a democratic way. Toward those ends, these by-laws have been conceptualized to provide for continuity and change as well as for efficiency and effectiveness as the faculty works cooperatively toward the purposes of the College.

PURPOSES

The College of Education at_____University shall:

- prepare personnel for professional teaching and leadership positions in a variety of educational institutions;
- contribute to the understanding of education as a body of knowledge;
- contribute to the development of institutional organizations and service systems to facilitate teaching and learning;

- provide leadership in effecting planned change in schools and colleges, particularly through efforts to close the theory-practice gap.

ORGANIZATION OF SUB-UNITS WITHIN THE COLLEGE

In order to achieve these purposes, members of the faculty of the College shall organize themselves into such departments as seem appropriate. Each department shall include eight or more regular faculty members, and shall present a statement of the purposes, organization, and functions of the sub-unit to the members of the faculty of the College which is consistent with the purposes, organization, and functions of the College and which will become the by-laws for that department if approved by a two-thirds majority of the members of the College or by such other official body as two-thirds of the faculty may direct.

Specifically, such a statement shall include: the name of the department; a description of the procedures for selecting an administrative head for that department; a delineation of the administrative head's duties and responsibilities; and a description of how the purposes of the department will be achieved, including a list of the curricular program plans and courses and a statement of the general research, service, and development activities for which the department intends to assume responsibility.

In organizing these departments, every member of the faculty of the College shall be a member of one and only one such unit. Every member of the faculty shall place himself in a department in which he feels most qualified to serve, provided that in cases in which the qualifications of members of any department be not agreed upon by all members of that department, such cases may be referred to the Faculty Council for final arbitration and decision. Centers, institutes, or other temporary task-force type, cross-unit groupings of faculty may also be formed from time to time to undertake specific projects, but these arrangements shall not constitute the basic departmental structure of the College, and the establishment of such groupings must be approved by the Faculty Council of the College.

Appendix B

ORGANIZATION OF THE COLLEGE

The College of Education at_____University shall include those regular faculty members assigned and budgeted to the College by the University. Plenary power shall rest with the faculty, which may convene itself in special session at any time for the purpose of conducting College business, provided that at least fifty per cent of the regular faculty members be in attendance.

There shall be established within the College a Faculty Council, an Executive Council, an Assessment Council, and a Student Council. The membership and structure of these councils are described below. No person shall be a voting member of more than one council.

Faculty Council

The Faculty Council of the College shall include elected representatives from the various departments of the College, provided that each department have one representative, and six representatives elected by the faculty of the College at large. Election of members shall be by secret ballot during the month of January every year, according to procedures established by the Faculty Council. Each member of the Council shall hold office for three years. Terms shall be staggered so that one-third of the representatives be elected to membership each year. Length of term for members of the initial Faculty Council shall be determined by lot. In the event of a vacancy, the Dean of the College shall appoint a representative from the appropriate department or from the faculty at large to fill that vacancy until the next regular election.

The Chairman of the Faculty Council shall be elected by the members of the Council on an annual basis each May. After his election, the administrative head of his department shall arrange it so that part of his load be allocated to his responsibilities as Chairman.

The Faculty Council shall establish permanent commissions on Graduate Studies, Undergraduate Program, Research and Development, Personnel, and Finance, and shall establish such other committees as may be necessary from time to time. Special committees which include teaching associates and other persons from outside the Council may be established by the Council, but a majority of the voting members on all commissions and committees shall be Council members, and the actions of all commissions and committees shall be reviewed and approved or disapproved by the Faculty Council.

Executive Council

The Executive Council of the College shall include the Dean and the administrative heads of each department of the College, who shall be selected according to the provisions of the by-laws of the University and the College and of each department of the College. The Dean shall serve as Chairman of the Executive Council. From time to time, there may be established service functions and offices under the direction of the Dean which shall include professional personnel from the various sub-units who shall be assigned to such offices for specified lengths of time and amounts of service, and whose assignment shall be made by the Dean and the other members of the Executive Council jointly.

Assessment Council

The Assessment Council of the College shall include five members appointed jointly by the Dean and the Faculty Council. Terms of office shall be for five years. No person shall be appointed to successive terms unless the initial appointment had been for a period of less than five years.

Appointments to the Assessment Council shall be made as follows: on July first of each even-numbered year, members of the Faculty Council shall appoint one man from a list of two persons presented to them by the Dean, and on July first of each odd-numbered year, the Dean shall appoint one man from a list of two persons presented to him by the Faculty Council, except that, initially, the Faculty Council shall appoint three persons from a list of six presented by the Dean, and the Dean shall appoint two persons from a list of four presented by the Faculty Council. Terms of office shall be staggered so that one

Appendix B 177

person's term shall expire each year. Length of term for members of the initial Assessment Council shall be determined by lot. In the event of vacancy, the Dean shall select one person from a list of two presented by the Faculty Council, and that person shall serve the remainder of the unexpired term.

The Chairman of the Assessment Council shall be appointed by the Dean to the Chairmanship for a period of two years, except that, initially, the appointment of a Chairman shall be made by the Dean during the year in which these by-laws are approved. The following year, the Dean shall appoint a Chairman-elect. Thereafter, the Dean shall appoint a Chairman-elect every two years, who shall serve in that capacity for one year and then serve as Chairman of the Assessment Council for a two-year period. Following his appointment as Chairman, it shall be arranged that part of his load be allocated to his responsibilities as Chairman. In addition, such other subordinate personnel as may be necessary to make such evaluations and studies as seem warranted shall also be assigned to the Assessment Council, and the Dean shall provide, through the authority of his office, for the Assessment Council to have access to such data in the pursuance of its tasks.

Student Council

Members of the Student Council of the College shall be elected by the students through their official organizations, or in whatever manner be deemed appropriate by the Faculty Council.

Membership in the Student Council shall be limited to seven juniors, eight seniors, and ten graduate students. Terms of office shall be for one year. Chairman of the Student Council shall be elected annually by members of that Council.

Assembly of Councils

At a formal faculty meeting each quarter, the various councils shall assemble and report publicly regarding their activities. These meetings shall be chaired by the Dean and considered open business meetings of the College after the official reports have been presented.

FUNCTIONS OF THE COUNCILS

In general terms, the Faculty Council shall be the policy-making body for the College, the Executive Council shall be the implementing and coordinating body for the College, the Assessment Council shall be the evaluating body for the College, and the Student Council shall represent the concerns of the student body to each of the various other councils.

Functions of the Faculty Council

The Faculty Council shall make policy and establish rules for the College within the framework of the by-laws of the University and the by-laws of the College. Official policy pertaining to programs, personnel, and budget shall be established by this council. Specifically, the Faculty Council shall establish policy regarding:

- faculty and student appointments;
- assignment to departments;
- procedures for creating new departments;
- centers or other task-force type, cross-unit groupings;
- admission standards and procedures for students;
- criteria for faculty promotion;
- faculty-load guidelines;
- allocation of resources;
- course offerings;
- program priorities;
- curricular requirements;
- procedures for reporting to the Assessment Council;

Appendix B 179

- such other factors as relate directly to the attainment of the purposes of the College.

The Council shall meet at least once each month from October through May, and on such other occasions as the Chairman may designate. The Council shall maintain an official record of its proceedings, including a summation of the decisions reached at each meeting, and this summation shall be distributed regularly and promptly to every member of the College faculty. Two-thirds of the members of the Council shall constitute a quorum. All meetings of the Faculty Council and sub-committees of that group shall be open to members of the faculty and students of the College, except those meetings which deal specifically with the activities or conduct of a given member of the faulty or constitute a hearing on a student case.

Functions of the Executive Council

Working with other members of the Executive Council, the Dean shall propose policy to the Faculty Council and he shall have the authority and responsibility to implement policy decisions which have been officially adopted by that body.

Specifically, the Dean shall make an annual presentation to the Assembly of Councils each fall in which he describes the progress of the College toward its goals and proposes new policy or changes in existing policy which he feels will be essential to attain those goals. The Dean or a representative of his choosing shall meet regularly with the Faculty Council but shall not have voting privieges in that body.

Functions of the Assessment Council

The Assessment Council shall function in such a way as to evaluate the effectiveness of the College in order to help it improve in its efforts to attain its purposes. Specifically, the Council shall function on the basis of reports of activities and progress which shall be submitted to it by the administrative heads of departments and the

Dean annually during the month of June or at such other times as reports may be requested, on the basis of reports formally lodged with the Assessment Council according to procedures set down by the Faculty Council, or on the basis of its own inquiry. The Council shall also serve as a review committee on recommendations regarding ranks and promotions for the College and shall submit its recommendations together with its evaluations directly to the Dean.

Since the basic purpose of the Assessment Council shall be to work toward the improvement of the College by converting concern, criticism, and empirical data into new information for the College to employ in increasing its effectiveness, the Council shall weigh and consider all information which may be presented to it or which it may request regarding the activities and policies of the College. The Assessment Council shall review the formal reports of the departments and the Dean, together with the six-year program plans, and shall report its findings to the faculty.

The Assessment Council shall have the authority to uphold or to negate the consistency of such activities and such policies with these by-laws, according to the judgment of a majority of its members. The Council shall also have the authority to sit as a Board of Appeals on any matter brought to it through proper channels by faculty, students, or any official body, and, following hearings and investigations, shall report its findings including actions contrary to these by-laws to the faculty.

The Assessment Council shall meet at least once each month from October through May, and on such other occasions as the Chairman may designate. The Council shall keep an official record of its proceedings, including a summation of the decisions reached at each meeting, and these summations shall be distributed quarterly to every member of the College faculty. The Council shall also publish at least once each year during the month of January, and at any other time of its own choosing, major reports of its efforts to evaluate the effectiveness of the various aspects of the College program. The Chairman of the Council or a representative of his choosing shall meet regularly with the Faculty Council but shall not have voting privileges in that body.

Functions of the Student Council

The function of the Student Council shall be to interpret the aspirations and the concerns of the student body in the College of Education to the Faculty, Executive, and Assessment Councils of the College. One graduate and one undergraduate representative from the Student Council shall meet regularly with each of the other councils of the College, except when their presence be considered inadvisable by a council chairman. Specifically, the Student Council shall make whatever program or other recommendations to the Faculty Council it feels merit consideration, make suggestions about and assist the Executive Council in the implementations of official College policy, and identify areas of strength and weakness and provide pertinent information regarding these areas of the College to the Assessment Council. The Student Council shall be especially sensitive to the concerns of those graduate students who serve as Teaching Associates or who otherwise function as junior members of the faculty and shall provide an official channel by which these concerns may be transmitted to the appropriate official or council.

ADOPTION AND REVISION OF THESE BY-LAWS

These by-laws shall become the official policy of the College of Education at_____University when approved by at least two-thirds of the regular members of the faculty of the College.

These by-laws may be amended or revised if two-thirds of the faculty of the College approve a specific proposal which had been previously approved by the Faculty Council or a proposal which had been formally presented to the Assembly of Councils on at least two consecutive meetings held during different quarters.

Appendix C

Establishing a Professional Practices Board

The membership of professional organizations within the field of education has traditionally had almost no experience in assessing the practices of members of their own professional group. University professors, public school teachers, flight instructors, corporation teachers—almost none of these or other educational groups deliberately discipline their own membership according to a statement of ethical or effectiveness principles such as various other professional groups attempt to do.

In the pages which follow is a suggested set of policies which is designed to enable the professional educators within a given school district to attempt to come to grips with the problem of unethical or ineffective practices by the members of their group. The statement represents a beginning effort, and would most certainly have to be modified theoretically and practically as conditions and experience allow. Unless educators assume responsibility for assessing their own members' actions, however, such assessments will necessarily be made by persons outside of the professional group. Society grants professional prerogatives only to those groups which demonstrate both a willingness and a capacity for restraining the unethical or ineffective practioneers within their own group. These suggested policies are intended as one short step in the direction of self-discipline and self-control.

Policies Affecting the Establishment and Function of a Professional Practices Board in _____ School District

The following policies relative to the establishment and function of a Professional Practices Board and Objectives Attainment Committee in _____ School District are hereby adopted. Included in these policies are statements of the assumptions upon which these groups are predicated, their organization and structure, and their function.

I. ASSUMPTIONS

1. Schools exist to help children learn:
   - to teach them how to learn;
   - to inspire them to learn;
   - to foster intelligent, democratic behavior.

2. The basic responsibility of educators is to facilitate such learning.

3. The efforts of educators can and must be continuously improved.

4. Members of the educational profession are the most competent judges of what is appropriate and what is inappropriate professional behavior.

5. In order to assure the highest quality of professional service, we engage ourselves, individually and collectively, to judge our colleagues and to be judged by them in accordance with the applicable provisions of the "Code of Ethics of the Education Profession."

II. ORGANIZATION

Local District

There shall be established within this school district the following organizational working committees:
- Active Building Committees;
- Building Objectives Attainment Committees;
- District Objectives Attainment Committee;
- Consideration Committee;
- Professional Practices Board.

The major purpose of this organizational structure shall be to facilitate communication among the various persons regarding professional behavior and to render judgments regarding same.

1. Each school building in the district shall have an Active Building Committee. This Committee shall be composed of three members. These members shall represent building teachers and shall meet the first Monday of the month at 4:00 P.M., or when called into special session by the chairman who shall be elected by the members of the group at their first meeting in January of each year. These meetings shall *not* be open to the public.

2. Each school building in the district shall have a Building Objectives Attainment Committee. This committee shall be composed of five members. These members shall be elected from each school building's teaching staff, and members shall serve for a two-year period of time. This group shall meet regularly the first Tuesday of each month at 4:00 P.M., or when called into special session by the chairman, who shall be elected by the members of the group at their meeting in January of each year.

3. The District Objectives Attainment Committee shall be composed of five members. These members shall be elected from among all of the educators within the district membership at large by secret ballot. Only persons who have served on the Building

Objectives Attainment Committee for at least two years may be eligible for election to this position. This group shall meet regularly the first Wednesday of each month at 4:00 P.M., or when called into special session by the chairman, who shall be elected by the members of the group at their first meeting in January of each year.

4. The Considerations Committee shall be composed of five members. These members shall be the current president of the District Education Association and the four most recent past presidents of the Association who are presently active within the organization. This group shall meet regularly on the second Monday of each month at 4:00 P.M., or when called into special session by the Chairman, who shall be elected by the members of the group at their first meeting in January of each year. *These meetings shall not be open to the public, and the topics of discussion and decisions reached shall be completely confidential.*

5. The Professional Practices Board shall be composed of nine or ten persons elected by the total membership of the District Education Association and representing the following groups:
   - 3 elementary teachers;
   - 3 secondary teachers;
   - 1 elementary principal;
   - 1 secondary principal;
   - 1 central office person;
   - 1 university representative (if there is a college or university within the district).

These members shall be elected by the groups which they represent. Members so elected shall remain in this position for three years. After the first election, terms of office shall be staggered so that no more than one-third of the membership of the Board shall be elected during any given year. The Professional Practices Board shall meet regularly on the second Tuesday of every month at 4:00 P.M. *These meetings shall not be open to the public, and the topics of discussion and decisions reached shall be completely confidential.*

III. FUNCTION

The major purpose of the Active Building Committee (ABC) shall be to review charges of unethical behavior and/or methods used for obtaining the educational objectives set forth in _____ School District.

1. These charges or requests for committee review may be made by any adult member of the _____ School District or by any other member of the educational community. These charges or requests must be submitted in writing to the Active Building Committee.

2. The members of the Active Building Committee shall review the charges or requests and must refer these problems to either the Building Objectives Attainment Committee or to the Considerations Committee. The referral shall be accompanied by the Active Building Committee's recommendation. This recommendation shall be considered by the other committee when making its decision.

Upon the recommendation of the Active Building Committee, the Building Objectives Attainment Committee shall review the written charges submitted to it regarding the methods or materials used to attain specific objectives in _____ School District and consider the recommendations made by the Active Building Committee.

1. A private hearing shall be scheduled to review the problem, at which time the educator involved shall be granted a hearing. The Building Objectives Attainment Committee shall render a decision and notify the educator and the individual who submitted the original request or charge of its decision.

2. The parties involved may appeal the decision to the District Objectives Attainment Committee within ten days.

The District Objectives Attainment Committee shall review cases sent to it by the Building Objectives Attainment Committee.

Appendix C

1. Upon the recommendation of the Active Building Committee, the District Objectives Attainment Committee shall consider charges or requests involving ways of attaining objectives in_____School District. This committee shall schedule a hearing and consider the evidence presented. *This shall be a private hearing.*

2. When a charge is submitted by the Building Objectives Attainment Committee, the Local Objectives Attainment Committee shall meet and review the written transcript obtained from the Building Objectives Attainment Committee hearing. This review shall occur only when one of the involved parties submits a written request for appeal within ten days after the Building Objectives Attainment Committee's decision. The local committee shall then have the opportunity to review the case and render its decision, which may or may not agree with the Building Objectives Attainment Committee's decision.

The major purpose of the Considerations Committee and the Professional Practices Board shall be to review charges of unprofessional conduct, and to render whatever judgments seem appropriate according to the provisions set forth below after considering the recommendation of the Active Building Committee.

1. Charges of unprofessional behavior may be made against any member of the professional group by any adult member of the_____School District or by any other member of the educational community. Such charges must be presented in writing to any member of the Considerations Committee or to the Active Building Committee.

2. The Considerations Committee shall function much in the same manner as a grand jury functions within the American legal system. This committee shall consider whether or not sufficient evidence of unprofessional behavior exists to warrant further investigation. In all of their deliberations, members of this group shall be dedicated to the proposition that students' growth and learning are paramount,

and they shall work in such a way so as to assure the attainment of that objective at all times. The members of the Considerations Committee shall be duty bound to present any charge of unprofessional behavior which has come to their attention. The Considerations Committee can only suggest that there seems to be sufficient reason for further professional investigation; therefore, its recommendation for further investigation and trial by the Professional Practices Board (1) does *not* constitute evidence of unprofessional behavior; (2) may be returned by a simple majority of the Considerations Committee; (3) does not guarantee the accused an opportunity to be present during the deliberations since he has not been charged with any wrongdoing. The Committee's failure to recommend further investigation does not ban such action by a subsequent group at some later time.

The Professional Practices Board shall hear charges of unprofessional behavior submitted to it by the Consideration Committee. A *private* hearing (i.e., not open to the public or other members of the profession) shall be held and the accused individual may be represented by legal counsel. The Professional Practices Board shall hear the evidence and render a decision on the basis of the evidence presented. An opportunity for appeal shall be given during a ten-day period following the decision. At this time, the Professional Practices Board shall report its recommendations to the _____ School Board.

IV. GENERAL

1. All hearings shall be private and the information obtained during these hearings shall be strictly confidential. At no time shall a member of a committee discuss the proceedings or testimony with any other person outside of the committee.

2. All charges or requests for review shall be submitted to the appropriate group in writing. Charges made verbally shall not be acted upon.

Appendix C

3. Any accused individual shall be entitled to counsel during any hearings at which his presence is required.

4. All committees shall meet at regularly scheduled times unless called into special session by the chairman.

Appendix D

Establishing Curriculum Research Councils

One way of evaluating the effectiveness of the educational endeavor is for a school district to establish a series of curriculum councils and charge them with the responsibility for improving the program by means of curriculum research. Formal adoption of such a set of policies, as is described in the following pages, commits a district to a program development and curriculum change effort which would be based on explicit assumptions and valid data.

There is nothing magic about curriculum councils; many districts have employed such councils ineffectively for years. The ideas described here have been employed successfully by a number of school districts, however, and they are made available as one more way in which educators can evaluate their activities carefully and creatively. Such a suggested set of policies should be considered as simply another approach to the problems and possibilities involved in assessing the effectiveness of education.

Recommended Policies Affecting the Establishment and Function of Curriculum Councils

The following policies relative to the establishment and function of a series of curriculum councils are hereby presented to the Board of Public Instruction for adoption as official policy. Included in these recommended policies are statements of the assumptions underlying curriculum councils, their organization and structure, and their function.

I. ASSUMPTIONS

1. Schools exist to help children learn.

2. Educational purposes can most effectively be realized by the organized instructional effort called curriculum.

3. The curriculum in our schools can be and must be continuously improved.

4. Curriculum consists primarily of what is commonly called subject matter and method. Both are important.

5. Many forces operate to affect curriculum (e.g., class size, availability of funds, number of books in the library, etc.), and they must be considered in any major effort to improve the curriculum.

6. To improve the curriculum, both the content of the various subject-matter fields and the methods whereby these facts and ideas are handled in a classroom must be improved.

7. The most effective way to bring about desirable change in the instructional program is to involve those persons who are most concerned with the curriculum: teachers, principals, parents, and wherever possible, students.

II. ORGANIZATION

There shall be established a District Curriculum Council and five different area curriculum councils. In addition, each school shall have a group whose responsibilities shall be directly related to improving the instructional program of that school. The major purpose of this organizational structure shall be to facilitate communication among the various persons concerned with the instructional program in the district's public schools.

1. The District Curriculum Council shall consist of twenty members representing various geographical, professional, and interest areas. This council shall meet monthly (or as the occasion demands) on the third Thursday of every month at 9:30 A.M. Further, this council shall elect a chairman and a vice chairman. The Director of Curriculum shall serve as secretary. Minutes of each meeting shall be distributed to each school, the superintendent, each school-board member, and such other persons as may be interested.

2. The membership of the District Curriculum Council shall be determined as follows:
   - four persons from each area curriculum council: *one* secondary school principal, *one* teacher, *one* elementary school principal, and *one* lay person;
   - the Director of Curriculum and such other members of his staff as he may feel should be included (ex officio).

Appendix D

3. Each area curriculum council shall include, wherever practical, a senior high school and all of its associated junior high schools and their feeder elementary schools. From these schools and their associated groups shall be developed area curriculum councils. Each area curriculum council shall include the following persons:
   - the principal of each school;
   - one teacher from each school;
   - one lay person from each school.

   Further, each area council shall elect a chairman and a secretary. Minutes of each meeting shall be distributed to each of the schools in that particular area and to the Director of Curriculum, who shall maintain a continuing file of the proceedings of each area council.

4. Schools shall be assigned to the following areas. Areas may be redefined and new schools assigned to appropriate areas at the discretion of the Director of Curriculum.

Area 1	*Area 2*	*Area 3*	*Area 4*	*Area 5*
North Side	South High	East High	West High	Central High
Lee JHS	Watson JHS	Jones JHS	Western JHS	Bailey JHS
Mason Street	Dillard JHS	Wetherby	Gratz	Martin JHS
Condord	Olympic	Burton	Thatcher	Morgan
Orange Lake	Hampshire	Bryson	McCollum	Hyde Park
Griffith	Jacobson	Eastwood		Moulton
Beechwood	Snyder			Ridenour
Templeton				

5. Each school shall have a curriculum council which shall work directly with the area curriculum council on matters of instruction. The size of these groups and their membership shall be left to the discretion of each school principal.

III. FUNCTION

The major purpose of each of the various curriculum councils shall be to improve instruction in the schools.

Further, their general method of operation shall be accomplished by means of research. That is, the various curriculum councils established here shall strive to cope with instructional problems either by systematically and comprehensively reviewing the pertinent published research reports, or by conducting experimental or other type research projects themselves, or both.

1. The District Curriculum Council shall function in the following manner:
    - isolate problems related to the curriculum in the public schools;
    - study these problems carefully through research;
    - make recommendations based upon these studies to the school board and such other groups as may be directly concerned.

2. The various area curriculum councils shall function in the following manner:
    - assist the District Council in identifying curriculum problems pertinent to the entire district. Further, each area curriculum council may also identify problems in instruction which are peculiar to that particular area for further study;
    - assist the District Council in carrying out its studies of the problems isolated for research. Further, each area curriculum council may also do research on the problems of instruction which are peculiar to that particular area;
    - assist the District Council in implementing those recommendations which are adopted.

3. Each school curriculum council shall function in the following manner:
    - assist the area curriculum councils in their efforts to help the District Curriculum Council identify instructional problems. Further, each school council may also identify problems in instruction which are peculiar to that particular school;
    - assist the area curriculum councils in their efforts to help the District Curriculum Council study instructional problems. Further, each school council may also do research on the problems of

Appendix D

instruction which are peculiar to that school;
- assist the area councils and the district councils implement those recommendations which are adopted.

Index

Academic respectability, 77
Action research, 14, 15
Administrative review, 67-68
Administrators, arbitrary, 74
Advisory committees, 40
Aftreth, Orville B., 87
Alder, Henry L., 87
Allen, Edward D., 87
Alter, Millicant, 88
Altmiller, W. R., 88
Altruism, 24-25, 42
America, 2, 6, 7, 31, 34
American Association for the Advancement of Science Committee on Science in the Promotion of Human Welfare, 33
American Federation of Teachers, 17
American Motors, 49
American Scientist, 31, 83
"American way," 3
Amidon, Edmund, 88, 89
Anderson, George, R., 89
Anderson, Kenneth E., 89
Anderson, Robert H., 89
Anti-Democratic Attitudes in American Schools, 39
Arthur, Grade, 90
Asher, William, 99
Assessment council, 70-73, 75
Assumptions, wrong, 24-25
"Attributes of a Profession," 78
Audio-lingual method, 43

Audio-visual aids, 14
Authoritarian control, 43, 44
Authority:
  bases, 79
  distribution, 82
Ax-Grinders: Critics of Our Public Schools, The, 9

Baden, Walter D., 90
Barrilleaux, Louis E., 90
Bateman, Donald, 91
Baxter, Joseph, 91
Beasley, Kenneth L., 91
Beery, Althea, 128
Behavioral objectives, 44
Behavioral science, 43
Beinharn, D. E., 92
Belcastro, Frank P., 92
Bell, Terrell Howard, 92
Bennett, Lloyd M., 92
Benschoter, Reba P., 93
Benson, Ronald L., 93
Berger, Irwin, 93
Better Business Bureau, 68
Bicak, L. J., 94
Bickel, Robert F., 94
Biersdorf, Kathryn Rooney, 94
Bingham, N. Eldred, 94
Biological Science Curriculum Study, 5, 13, 18
Bjelke, Joan, 114
Blake, Robert W., 95
Blankenship, Jacob Watson, 95
Blesh, T. Erwin, 95

Blickenstaff, Channing B., 96
Blocher, Clyde E., 151
Blocher, Don H., 93
Bloomenshine, L. L., 96
Boeck, Clarence H., 97
Bollenbacker, Joan K., 128, 129
Bowman, Herman J., 97
Boyd, Claude Collins, 97
Brandon, James Rodger, 97
Brown, B. Frank, 98
Brown, Malcomb T., 96
BSCS, 5, 13, 18
Bucher, Charles, 98
Buildings, changed, 18
Bundy, E. Wayne, 99
Burkey, Betty, 99
Burnett, MacCurdy, 99

Caldwell, Loren T., 99
Calia, V. F., 115
Cantrell, Sue Rowe, 99
Carbone, Robert F., 100
Carpenter, Paul W., 100
Cassel, Russell N., 100
Castens, Anne Cole, 101
Catcher in the Rye, 37
Caution, factor in change, 76
Cawelti, Gordon, 18
CBA, 13
Censors and the Schools, The, 9
Certificate, temporary, 25
Certification, 17
Champa, V. Anthony, 101
Change:
   propositions for, 62-83
   social, 31-35
   theoretical model, 46-61
Changing Values in College, 39
Charles, Don C., 93
CHEM, 13
Chemical Bond Approach, 13
Chemical Education Material Study, 13
Chicago, 7
Child-centered schools, 43
China, 3

Chrysler Corporation, 49
"Cities-What Next, The," 6
Civil War, 2, 35
Claye, Clifton M., 101
Clements, Barton E., 101
Closed system, 40, 70
Coffield, William H., 102
Cogan, Morris L., 102
Collective Negotiations for Teachers: An Approach to School Administration, 17
College, 73
Commager, Henry Steele, 9
Commitment, 76
Commoner, Barry, 33, 83
Communist nations, 3, 4
Competence, bases for authority, 79
Computer-based teaching machines, 14
Condra, James Bruce, 102
Confidence, system dimension, 50-54, 58-59
Congress, 34, 40
Consolidation, 14
Constitution of the United States, 82
Consultants, 41
Content, change hypotheses, 12-13
Control, educational dilemma, 41, 42-44
Coon, Lewis Hubert, 103
Cooperative Research Program of U.S. Office of Education and National Institutes of Mental Health, 16
Core program, 14
Corwin, Edward S., 82
Cousins, Jack E., 103
Cowan, Paul Jackson, 103
Cox, C. Benjamin, 104
Criticism, 82-83
Crumb, Glenn Howard, 104
Curriculum changes, 18
Curriculum council, 14

Index

"Curriculum Reform," 21
Curriculum research, 81
Curriculum revision, 5
Cyphert, Frederick R., 104

Dandes, Herbert M., 105
Davis, Edward A., 105
Day, William W., 105
Dean, Stuart E., 106
Decision-making, involvement in, 15
Deitz, James Emery, 106
de facto segregation, 7
DeGraft, Homer R., 106
Demonstration programs, 6
Dempsey, Richard Allen, 106
Department of Agriculture, 6
Department of Defense, 6
Department of Labor, 6
Descriptive studies, 15
Dewey, 15
Diagnostic testing, 14
Discipline, 42
DNA, 13
Dodd, Senator, 68
Doing, system concept, 29-30, 36, 40
Dolan, G. Keith, 107
Domain, system dimension, 47, 48-49, 57-58
Donelly, Edward Joseph, 107
Drexler, Henry Edward, 107
Driscoll, John P., 108
Dropouts, 15
Dunn-Rankin, Peter, 160
Dyer-Bennett, John, 108

Ebert, Mary Gertrude, 108
Economic questions, 22
Educational domains, 57-60
Educational innovation, 5
Educational Research Information Centers, 6
Educational system, reconceptualizing, 53-60
Educational television, 14, 18, 19, 23
Education as a Profession, 17, 78
Education of Teachers, The, 17
Effectiveness, 22-23, 42
Eigen, Lewis D., 109
Elementary and Secondary Education Act of 1965, 5
Elsmere, Robert T., 109
Ends and means, 81
Enzmann, Arthur Milton, 109
ERIC, 6
ESEA, 5
Ethical code, 42
Ethics, professional, 79
ETV, 20
External variables, 23
Extremist activities, 4, 8-9
Evaluating, 30-31, 36-41, 43
Evaluation, 81
Evaluative function, 65-70
Evidence of change, 18
"Evolving a Theory of Effectiveness in Education," 79
Expert judgement, 87

Faculty Participation in Academic Governance, 75
Failures, educational change, 20-25
Farley, Eugene S., 109
Farley, John J., 110
Federal involvement, 4-6
Feedback, 32-34, 41, 68, 81, 82-83
Ferris, Frederick L., Jr., 110
Field study, 14
"Fifth-Year" program, 17
Fillmer, J. T., 100, 110
Finder, Glen E., 110
First Amendment to the Constitution of the United States, 34
Fisk, W. W., 111
Flanders, N., 88, 111, 112

FLES, 13
Ford Motor Company, 49
Foreign language, 4, 5, 18
Foreign Language Elementary School, 13
Forgetting, 15
Foundations, 17
Franklin, 12
Freedom, Loyalty, Dissent, 9
Free will, denial, 44
French, J. W., 112
French, Lillian A., 112
Frequency questions, 20-22
Friebel, Allen Cahoun, 112
Friedman, Robert, 112
Fry, Edward B., 113
Frye, Charles H., 113
Frymier, Jack R., 66, 78
Fuller, William R., 108
Fulmer, Earl Ray, 113
Function, system dimension, 49-50, 58
Future of Public Education, The, 17

Gagné, Robert M., 114
Garside, Leonard J., 114
Gellhorn, Walter, 67, 68
General Electric, 49
General practioner, 77
Geneva Disarmament Talks, 4
Georgiades, William, 114
Giammateo, Michael, 89
Gibson, R. E., 115
Gibson, Robert L., 116
Glad, Joan Rogers Bourne, 115
Glanz, Edward, 115
Glennon, Vincent J., 115
Goal:
  educational, 44, 54-57
  process type, 15
  system dimension, 47-48, 54-57
Gold, Joy Rochell, 116
Goldberg, Miriam L., 116
Goodlad, John I., 117

Goodman, Thomas L., 117
Goodwin, William L., 135
Gottschulk, Bunther H., 117
Grade level, 25
Grading, 25
Gragg, Irene A., 118
Grassell, Edward Milton, 118
Grassmeyer, Donald Leroy, 118
Greenwood, Ernest, 78
Grobman, Hulda, 118, 119
Groff, Frank H., 119
Gropper, George L., 120
Grotberg, Edity, 120
Grote, Charles Nelson, 121
Group dynamics, 14
Grouping, 14, 15, 23
Group interaction, 15
Group relations, democratic, 15
Grubb, Betty Sayre, 121
Guidance programs, 5
Guilford, J. P., 121

Halliwell, Joseph W., 121
Hamilton, Mary Una, 122
Harous, Delbert, 122
Hart, Richard H., 122
Harvard, 12
Hayman, John L., 122, 123
Hedlund, Dalva E., 146
Hemphill, John K., 123
Henderson, Clara A., 123
Hendrix, Oscar R., 124
Herminghous, Earl G., 124
Hillson, Maurie, 124
Higher education, changing, 73-75, 76
Hipsher, Warren L., 124
Hoban, Pierce F., 125
Hoepfner, Ralph, 121
Homeostatic mechanisms, 35
Homework, 14
Honig, Jurgen M., 156
Hopkins, Kenneth D., 125
Houston, William Robert, Jr., 125
Howell, Wallace J., 125

Index

Huettig, Alice, 126
Huggett, Albert J., 17, 78
Hughes, Marie, 126
Human relations, 14
Hunt, Edward G., 126
Hunt, Ronald Leroy, 127
Huntinger, Paul, 127

Ideologies, 2, 3-4
Ikeda, Hirochi, 127
Independent study, 14
Industrial arts, 18
Initial Teaching Alphabet, 14
Innovation in education, 5
"Innovative Practices in High Schools: Who Does What—and Why—and How," 18
Input factors, 81-82
Inservice education, 15, 16
Inservice study groups, 14
Instructional materials, 15
Integrity, 63-65
Integrity of science, 82-83
"Integrity of Science," 83
Integrity of Science: A Report by the AASA Committee on Science in the Promotion of Human Welfare, The, 30
Interaction analysis, 14
Internship, 17
Isaiah 33:22, 63
ITA, 14, 20

Jackson, Joseph, 128
Jacob, Philip, 39
Jacobs, James N., 128, 129
Jacobson, Harvey K., 166
Janes, Robert W., 129
Jantzen, Victor W., 129
Jefferson, 51
Jensen, Lawrell, 130, 147
Jerman, Max, 100
Jessell, John C., 130
Johnson, James, 122, 123
Johnson, Robert H., 130
Jones, Emlyn, 131

Jones, Reginald, 91
Judgements, 42
Judgement, expert, 81
Judicial review, 67
Justman, Joseph, 116, 131

Keating, Raymond F., 131
Kemp, C. Gratton, 131
Kenney, Clifford, 135
Klaus, David J., 132
Klauser, Eva L., 132
Klausmeier, Herbert J., 132
Kleinman, G. K., 17
"Knowledge: A Growth Process," 82
Knowledge explosion, 2, 3
Knox, Donald Waser, 133
Koontz, W. F., 133
Kraft, Charles H., 133
Krumboltz, John D., 133, 134
Kumata, Hideya, 134
Kusinitz, Ivan, 135

Lambert, Philip, 135
Lance, Mary Louise, 135
Landis, Carl, 136
Language, foreign, 4, 5
Language laboratories, 14, 19, 43
Large-group instruction, 14
Lawson, Fred Russell, 136
Lax, John E., 136
Lay committees, 15
Leadership, 14-15
Learning, 15
Lefever, D. Welty, 125
Legal authority, role in policy decision, 81
Legal question, 22
Legislative review, 68
Leinwold, Judith, 128
Leles, Sam, 79
Leutnegger, Ralph R., 136
Library procurement, 3, 6
Lieberman, Myron, 17, 78
Lisonbee, Lorenzo K., 137
Literature, 18

Livingston, Howard F., 137
Lobb, M. Delbert, 130
Local control, 41, 42-43
Logical significance, 19
Loman, M. LaVerne, 137
Lonsdale, Bernard J., 138
Lorge, Sarah W., 138
Loretan, Joseph O., 138
Lovell, J. T., 138
Lowe, William T., 139
Luckie, William Ronald, 139
Lumsdaine, Arthur A., 120
Lyman, L., 169

MacEachern, Donald G., 87
Mahler, F. L., 141
Malan, June R., 141
Markland, S., 142
Marks, Edmond, 142
Marshall, Lorene, 138
Martin, Gaither Lee, 142
Marxist-Leninist point of view, 3
"Master of Arts in Teaching," 17
Mathematics, 4, 18
McCallon, Earl L., 139
McCarthy, Senator, 68
McFarlon, Robert O., 140
McGarvey, Paul, 140
McKinney, Max Terral, 140
McManus, Barry, 125
McNeil, John, 141
Meacham, Ester A., 143
Means and ends, 81
Melaragno, Ralph J., 143
Melton, R. S., 149
Meranda, Peter F., 143
Merkley, Philip, 130
Methodological change hypotheses, 14
Methods, 15, 77
Middle school, 14
Mikkelson, J. C., 143
Mills, D. L., 78
Mitchell, James V., 144
Mitchell, Virginia White, 144
Montgomery, Fred S., 89
Moore, Patricia, 144

Moore, Sid F., 89
Morris, Ruby Pearl, 145
Moses, John Irving, 145
Moskow, Michael H., 17
Mueller, Theodore H., 136
Mullin, Daniel W., 145
Myers, Robert B., 146

Nance, Afton D., 146
Nasca, Donald, 146
National Defense Education Act of 1958, 4
National Education Association, 15
National Institutes of Health, 6, 16
National Science Foundation, 5
Nation's Schools, 18
Nature of Educational Method, The, 78
NCAA, 31
NDEA, 5, 43
NEA, 17
Negotiations, professional, 17
Negro, 6, 7
Neidt, Charles O., 146
Nelson, Ester, 146
Nelson, Jack, 9
Nesbitt, William Otto, 147
Newell, John M., 126
New York State Board of Regents, 43
Noall, Matthew F., 147
Nongraded school, 14
Norton, Donald A., 87
NSF, 5, 43

Objectives, 44
Ofman, William, 148
Ohio State Law Journal, 66
Oldridge, Buff, 148
Olson, Lowell Ellis, 148
Ombudsman, 68
Ombudsman and Others in Nine Countries, 68
Orderly change, 34-35
    change hypotheses, 13-14

Index

professional, 78-81
Organizational structure,
  professional, 80
Osburn, H. G., 149
Ottina, John R., 154
Outline of History, The, 9
Over, Charles H. R., 142

Paige, Donald Dean, 149
Passow, A. H., 116
Pella, Milton O., 149, 167
Perkins, Hugh, 149
Perkins, John A., 82
Personnel, change hypotheses, 16
Peterson, Hugh, 121
PFDA, 67
Philosophical significance, 19
Physical education, 18
Physical Science Study
  Committe, 5, 12
Physics, 18
Planning, 29, 40
Platt, John R., 50
Popham, W. James, 150
Population explosion, 2-3
Potter, Van Rensselaer, 81
Poulos, Chirs, 149
Power:
  real, 41
  role change, 34
Preamble, U. S. Constitution, 47
Prediction, 43-44
Pre-service training, 78
President, the, 29, 34, 51
Programmed instruction, 14, 18, 19
Professionalism, 17, 41, 42
"Professionalism in Context," 66
Professionalization, 78
*Professional Negotiation in
  Public Education,* 17
Professional posture, 66-67
*Professional Problems of
  Teachers,* 17, 78
Professional status, 76-81
Profession of Teaching, The, 17
Project English, 5, 13

Project method, 14
Project Social Studies, 5, 13
Project Talent, 5
PSSC, 5, 12, 18, 19, 20, 21, 22
PTA, 7
Pure Food and Drug
  Administration, 67
Public education, changing,
  70-73, 76
Public interest in schools, 4, 7-8

Rabkin, Lezlie Y., 150
Raywid, Mary Anne, 9
Reading teaching methods, 23
Record dimension, 59-60
Redundance, 65-70
Regional laboratories, 6
Remmers, H. H., 39
*Report of the National Advisory
  Commission on Civil
  Disorders,* 6
Research, 5, 15-16
Retention in grade, 15
Rice, Jimmy Marshall, 150
Richardson, Richard E., 151
Richman, Paul Tobias, 151
Riggle, Wanda B., 130
Roberts, Jr., Gene, 9
Rollins, Sidney P., 151
Rose, Gale, 147
Rosenbloom, Paul C., 152
Rothney, John W. M., 130, 143
Rottmann, Leon H., 152
Roughead, William George, 152
Ruddell, Arden K., 153
Rudy, Rhoda, 130
Russell, David R., 153
Russian Revolution, 3

Sanctions, 17
Sandefur, Joseph T., 153
Saturday Review, 82
Sawyer, Robert Lee, 154
Sax, Gilbert, 154
Schiffman, Gilbert B., 154
Schiller, Mary Philomene, 155

Schmieding, Orville A., 155
School Mathematics Study
  Group, 5, 12
School study group, 14
Scholz, Alfred, 95
Schroeder, Wade W., 134
Schuff, Robert V., 155
Schuster, Edgar H., 155
Science, 21, 33, 81, 82
Science, 4, 18, 43-44, 50
"Science and Human Survival," 33
"Science and the Race Problem," 33
Seeman, Melvin, 156
Segregation, 7
Sequin, Edmond L., 158
Seibert, Warren F., 108, 156
Self-discipline, 17
Senate, 34, 51
Sensitivity training, 14
Service, 42
Shaevitz, Morton, 148
Shanks, Merrill E., 108
Sharkan, William W., 156
Sherman Anti-Trust Act, 68
Shuff, Robert W., 167
Siess, Thomas F., 165
Significance, 19
Silagyi, Dezo V., 157
Skills, 77
Slaichert, William M., 157
Small-group discussion, 14
Smith-Lever Act, 12
Smith-Hughes Act, 12
Smith, Frederick R., 157
Smith, Gene, 115
SMSG, 5, 12, 19
Social change, 31-35
Social revolution, 4, 6-7, 9-10
Social systems concept, 27-31
Social Work, 78
"Society and Science," 81
Somit, Albert, 158
Soviet Russia, 3
Spencer, R. C., 158

Spencer, Richard E., 158
Sputnik, 4
State education assessment council, 70-73
State House Conference on Education, 56
Statistical significance, 19
Stephens, Jr., Marion L., 157
Stevens, Deon Orlo, 158
Stewart, John W., 159
Stickell, David W., 159
Stinnett, T. M., 17, 78
Storlie, Theodore R., 159
Strikes, 17
"Strong Inference," 50
Sub-systems, 68-70
Supervision, 10, 16
Supreme Court, 34, 51
Sutman, Frank X., 160
Swanson, Lloyd G., 130
Sweet, Raymond, 160
System:
  closed, 70
  education, 72, 81-83
  integrity, 64
  sub-systems, 68-70
  university, 73-75

Taddonio, Dominik, 98
Taffel, Alexander, 160
Tallent, John B., 160
Taylor, Bob L., 161
Teacher-education, 16
Teacher-pupil planning, 14
Teachers, preparing, 76
Teacher-training institutions, 17
Teacher turnover, 15
Teaching machines, 14
Teaching methods, 15
Team teaching, 13-14, 18, 19
Technical education, 43
Techniques, 77
Temporary certificates, 25
Television, educational, 14, 18, 19, 23

Index

Term papers, 77
Testing, diagnostic, 14
Thelen, H. A., 161
Theorizing, 29
"Third party" ideas, 75
Thomson, Scott D., 161
Thorndike, 15
Tower, Melvin M., 162
Tradition, 76, 81
Transfer, 15
Traweek, Melvin W., 162
Trotter, Charles Earl, 162
Troutner, Howard LaVerne, 162
Trowbridge, Leslie Walter, 163
Traux, Robert Lloyd, 163
Trustees, 74

Ulrich, John H., 163
United Nations, 3, 4
United States, 2, 18, 42, 68
United States Office of Education, 5, 16
Unit method, 14
University, 73-75
USOE, 5, 16
U. S. Office of Education, 15

Vance, Kenneth, 164
VanderMeer, Abram W., 89
Varenhorst, Barbara, 133
Variables, 23-24
Vested interest, 76
Vocational education, 18, 43
Vollmer, H. M., 78

Walker, Jerry L., 164
Walsh, John, 21

Walter, Dick, 114
Walters, Louis, 164
Warnken, Robert G., 165
Watts, 7
Weber, Arnold R., 75
Weber Report, 75
Wedemeyer, C. A., 167
Weiss, Paul, 82
Wells, H. G., 9
West, Jesse W., 165
West, LeRoy C., 165
Westinghouse, 49
Westley, Bruce H., 166
When Americans Complain, 67
"Which College is Best?" 82
White, Robert H., 166
White, Robert William, 166
White House Conference on Education, 56
Wiersma, William, 132, 135
Wiley, Frank A., 166
Williams, Emmet D., 167
Wittich, W. A., 167
Woerdehuff, Frank J., 96
Wolfe, Frank A., 167
Working conditions, teacher, 15
Wright, Robert Earl, 168

Yost, Michael, 160
Yourd, John L., 168

Zahn, Richard D., 168
Zidonis, Frank, 91
Ziebarth, Raymond Allan, 169
Zimmerman, Helen, 169
Zweibelon, I. M. Bahmuller, 169